CW01668680

JANET HUTCHINSON is a writer and editor. She taught creative writing for many years in community and tertiary education settings, mostly at the University of Technology, Sydney. Her fiction and non-fiction have been published in various magazines, literary journals and anthologies, and her short stories are collected in *Desire and Other Domestic Problems*. She lives and works in Sydney.

Grandma Magic

TRUE STORIES BY AND ABOUT GRANDMOTHERS

EDITED BY **JANET HUTCHINSON**

ALLEN&UNWIN

First published in 2009

Copyright © Janet Hutchinson 2009
Copyright for each individual story remains with the Contributor of that story.

All rights reserved. No part of this book may be reproduced or transmitted in any form or by any means, electronic or mechanical, including photocopying, recording or by any information storage and retrieval system, without prior permission in writing from the publisher. The *Australian Copyright Act 1968* (the Act) allows a maximum of one chapter or 10 per cent of this book, whichever is the greater, to be photocopied by any educational institution for its educational purposes provided that the educational institution (or body that administers it) has given a remuneration notice to Copyright Agency Limited (CAL) under the Act.

Allen & Unwin
83 Alexander Street
Crows Nest NSW 2065
Australia
Phone: (61 2) 8425 0100
Fax: (61 2) 9906 2218
Email: info@allenandunwin.com
Web: www.allenandunwin.com

Cataloguing-in-Publication details are available from the National Library of Australia.

ISBN 978 1 74175 684 5

Internal Design by Gayna Murphy, Greendot Design
Set in 13/16 pt Bembo by Midland Typesetters, Australia
Printed and bound in Australia by Griffin Press

10 9 8 7 6 5 4 3 2 1

For my mother, Heather

CONTENTS

Introduction

JANET HUTCHINSON

WHEN I THINK of grandmothers the notion that often springs to mind is that of legacy—a gift or bequest, something that is passed on, or handed down. We may have been bestowed with a grandmother's name, or we're endowed with one or more of her physical features—the shimmer across a cheek, the cast of a brow, the turn of an ankle, the rise of a bosom, piano-playing fingers. Perhaps we've inherited something of our grandmothers' other attributes, personality traits—a propensity for survival, a prevailing generosity of spirit, a predisposition to frugality. Maybe we've taken on an attitude to the world that betrays itself in cantankerous ways, or possibly we share a contrary sense of humour.

Our grandmothers—wittingly or not—may have bequeathed us with any number of handy skills and talents, including domestic ones: a light hand when it comes to scones and sponge cakes, a deftness with knitting needles or a crochet hook, the knack for the necessary calm before the potential terrors of an electric sewing machine. Somewhere, surely, we have stashed that hand-scribbled recipe for nectarine conserve or foolproof champagne pastry. They may have passed on their passions—an abiding interest in current affairs, an inextinguishable attachment to books, the longing for song, the love of a good yarn. If we are lucky we have been the beneficiaries of scraps of wisdom, a few simple words we cling to, talismans that will help get us through the trickiest of times.

Sometimes a grandmother's legacy is something much more tangible—a marcasite brooch, a strand of pearls, an opal ring. We may have made room in our households for some of her former possessions—a crystal vase, a delicate pink demi-tasse and its matching saucer, a pure linen tea towel just for drying glasses, a pastel landscape in oils, the page of an old newspaper from the war containing a telling item that had caught the eye. And of course we are often left with abiding memories—chuckles over a cuppa or a tumbler of cordial, walks along the beach on the lookout for pretty shells, snatched moments in the backyard marvelling at a gardenia or frangipani coming into bloom. We remember the extended phone conversations with the tennis commentary humming in the background, exchanged cards, the occasional scrawled letter.

When I think of my own grandmothers two images remain especially potent. Not so surprisingly perhaps, they place each in her kitchen, at her fading formica table: one completely unflustered by the continual comings and goings across the lino, cochineal-icing a not-long-out-of-the-oven slice before deftly sprinkling it with desiccated coconut and explaining to me as she did so the meaning of the word 'camouflage'; the other rummaging through bundles of tattered yellowed envelopes tied with satin ribbon, muttering indecipherable phrases under her breath all the while and, sadly, not opening a single one of them to allow me to catch even a glimpse of its contents.

And then there are all the lingering stories—or at least the precious, twinkling fragments of them. But this is only what thinking about grandmothers conjures up for me.

I FIRST ENVISAGED THIS ANTHOLOGY some time back when, completely out of the blue it seemed, people began asking me if I was a grandmother yet. I recall being quite taken aback by this at the time—I was so young, after all!—but it got me thinking. Not only about the grandmothers in my life, but about grandmothers and grandmothering more generally: the intrinsic nature of the relationship, the supposed role; any attendant allure; the assumptions, the expectations and the pressures, be they personal, familial, societal or otherwise. What had prompted this disarming question, I wondered. Perhaps something vital had eluded me along the way.

And then a year or so ago, at a wake, someone I hadn't seen for a long while, with adult children around the same age as mine, asked not if I had grandchildren, but if I *wanted* any. She posed her query quietly and I confided my response equally sotte voce; given the exceptionally sad circumstances of this funeral it would have been more than unseemly to do otherwise. But the upshot for me was the arousal of a further, deeper curiosity. By now the stuff of desire had come into it.

Still, I was more intrigued than ever. I became eager to find out if others had done much thinking in and around this subject. Did anyone else feel the way I did? Inquisitive as ever, I was after the odd answer or so. But I was prepared to wait for them. I didn't necessarily want the sorts of responses that can be so readily dished out in the glossies or on the telly. In the meantime, I was content to just mull things over. But the spark ignited soon began to flare.

LIKE MANY PEOPLE, especially when it involves a search for insights pertaining to significant emotional relationships, I glean critical—and treasured—knowledge from reading; this is but one way we learn about the world, and how others set about to live in it. So when I began commissioning pieces for this anthology I hoped not only that they'd let me in on a few mysteries, but that they might give voice to a wide range of actual lived experiences.

I held my breath. I anticipated some good grandma yarns, some enthralling nanna stories, any number of which might put a different spin on the tired images the media is so often inclined to deliver. I hoped to the heavens that the contributions would be neither preachy nor proselytising. I was keen for the book not to be prescriptive. Frankly, I was up for a few fresh perspectives. Simply by virtue of what was told, I trusted that the submitted work might allow some perusal of this subject in a manner which was neither inappropriately romanticising nor unduly sentimental.

Because the truth is, grandmothers are a motley lot. Although they are often portrayed in the popular imagination as somehow saintly and unswervingly devoted to their grandchildren, and while it can be way too easy to pop each and everyone of them on a pedestal, in reality—for better or worse, just like the rest of us—women who are grandmothers are neither replete with moral goodness and the milk of human kindness to the last, nor all of them paragons of piety and patience. Indeed, they can even be quite wicked, in their own idiosyncratic ways. There is, after all, no single prescription for being a grandmother—or mother, for that matter—just as there is no definitive experience of having a grandmother or more in your life.

I COULD HAVE OPTED to canvass the thoughts and recollections of my age-peers alone, baby-boomers, the ones currently becoming grandmothers. But I was intent on casting my net further. I wanted to hear what women both younger and older had to say. Would I be blessed with truthful accounts, recalcitrance, or both? By some stroke of fortune, I got much more than I bargained for. From the outset I was struck by the candour—and indeed the ardour—with which contributors embraced the subject I'd flung their way. One by one—be it by means of memoir, personal essay, or some entrancing, entwining blend of these forms—a range of bewitching takes on the matter began to emerge, each in its own way getting under the veneer of the more usual depictions of grandmothers and grandmothering. The sparkling suite of stories I'd allowed myself to imagine began to materialise.

Each piece was thoughtful, well-considered, this was immediately clear. But each also had carved a beguiling path of its own around and beyond my brief; each took me somewhere I hadn't really anticipated. Certainly, I had not entirely expected that contributors would delve so deep, hauling all manner of enchanting titbits and hitherto unknown, unexplored scraps of information to the surface of their narratives. Compiling this anthology felt like being a party to any number of tantalising discoveries. It was exciting, fascinating, albeit at times discomforting, turning the pages to see what spellbinding detail had been uncovered. I was thrilled to bits.

THIS ANTHOLOGY BRINGS TOGETHER twenty new pieces of writing by Australian women. These contributors come from diverse backgrounds and live in disparate places and situations. They range widely in age as much as in outlook. Some of them are grandmothers; others are not. But whatever the case, whether by way of a tightly structured telling or somewhat more reflective meditation, all have let us in—and many with great affection, a good number through moments of rollicking humour—on the oft-times quirky, quizzical world of grandmothering.

Some of these grandmothers act in unexplained, even unexpected ways; many manage—in spite of all sorts of otherwise inexcusable behaviours—to retain a compelling, irresistible charm. We meet grandmothers who surreptitiously introduce their grandchildren to some of the more intricate workings of the world; others are clearly besotted and may even indulge their grand offspring shamelessly. Some, in their dotage, plot and scheme to set situations right. Others are alert to the risks inherent in interfering and do what they can to stay well out of the way, and out of the limelight.

There are meek grandmotherly women in these stories, as much as bossy, outspoken ones. There are stern, strict grandmothers who rule the roost if not the entire clan, just as much as there are easy-going, laid-back ones, women still perfectly able to roll with the punches. We become acquainted with a number of grand women who have been largely disregarded for much if not all of their lives, even more so in their declining years. And we get to meet strong, resolute women who have carved a place of their own in this country's history; some of them have achieved public recognition in their own right, for their own considerable achievements, however humbly they may perceive them. All are conjured up here, on these pages, in these words. And among them is one grandmother whose legacy, by virtue of an arresting stroke of forethought, is truly magic.

She Says: Naming and Grandmother Magic

KRISTINA OLSSON

SHE SAYS, *you're my best friend*. She says, *don't interrupt me when I'm drawing*. And *I'm the driver. You sit there and put your seatbelt on, my girl*.

I WAS NAMED FOR KRISTINA, my father's mother. I didn't meet her until I was seventeen, when we stayed for two months in her village in southern Sweden. For my whole childhood I had imagined her, this woman whose name I had, at the same time imagining myself into the name. As a small child I didn't have much to go on, but even then, from stories and photos, I knew I would have to be brave, intrepid even, independent, strong. I tried hard. I didn't want to let my grandmother down.

My mother's mother, Veronica, was feisty and lively too. Short and wiry, she loved to dance and to sing, with a clamorous voice and working-class vowels only a fishwife could envy. She was Australian by birth, nature and habit: plain-spoken, open and a gambler. She'd bet on anything from the chocolate wheel to the day of a baby's birth.

Veronica was fun to be around but she grew old too quickly, convincing herself of the gravity of age when she was scarcely out of her fifties. She seemed to simply deflate. At fifty-five she declared she was too old for Christmas, at sixty-five too weary to leave the house. Despite this she was in rude health into her seventies, and even then she seemed to *imagine* herself unwell, to have talked herself into it. Well, she'd mothered seven children in bleak times, she was probably just dead tired.

Kristina, on the other hand, tall and lean, mother of two sons, rode in the local village bicycle race until she was eighty. Was a passenger on one of the first flights from Sweden across the North Pole to America, where she visited her brother August in Idaho. Holidayed regularly in Majorca, with or without my grandfather. She would send photos: she and her women friends taking the sun beneath palm trees, large sunglasses disguising their enjoyment. My father loved these photos, proof of his mother's fierce independence, her fearlessness. Despite the physical distance that separated them, and the discipline she'd meted out when he was young, he adored her. I could tell by the tone he used as he translated her letters and cards for us. I loved that. He'd given me the name of someone he *adored*.

SHE ARRIVES CLUTCHING A SOFT TOY, in a dress that billows above scratched boots, hair startled into erratic curls behind her. Sometimes she shoulders a pink backpack containing everything important: her juice, her bear, a vitamin pill she's stolen from her mother. A purple bracelet. A fifty-cent piece. Her name is Amber, and she's three. We see each other briefly several times a week, but on Thursdays we get to hang out all day. We pretend to eat breakfast, but there are better things: tomatoes, kiwi fruit, olives, cup cakes. We drink tea from miniature pastel cups; she raises hers to mine and says *cheers!*

FEW PEOPLE in my extended family are known by their given names. This may have something to do with my parents: when he came to Australia my father halved his given name, Kjell-Arne, for obvious reasons, and is known as Arne. My mother, named Veronica for her own mother, was known mainly as Yvonne all her adult life. This may have been to differentiate mother and daughter, but I don't think so. At any rate, when she wasn't Yvonne she was Mimi. The adults around her used Mimi as a name, but my children used it as a title. *She's my Mimi*, they would say by way of introducing her. They would refer to other grandmothers in the same way—as *Sarah's Mimi* or *Heidi's Mimi*. My mother thought this quaint and wonderful, even when it was shortened, as Australian names inevitably are, to Mim.

Similarly, within my family I am not Kristina or Kristine but Kiki. Even to my children. I suppose I expected my grand-daughter to pick it up too—it seemed a fine name for a grandmother, and easy to say—but things have turned out differently. When she was forming her first words, my son and his wife taught her some basic Swedish words. One of them was *Farmor*—father's mother—the name I used for my Swedish grandmother. Amber's earliest attempts at this produced *Wawa*. Now, years later, that's who I am.

SOMETIMES SHE DOESN'T WANT TO TALK. The air is thick with her lumpy, wordless protest. She says, finally, *don't look at me!* or *my dress is* not *pretty!* and marches into another room or out onto the verandah, where Charlotte and her expanding silvery web always distract and calm her. *Good morning Charlotte*, she says sternly on these mornings, her nose creasing with the same frown she wore when she was born.

ON THAT FIRST TRIP to Sweden, thirty-five years ago, I think I was looking for confirmation that I could live up to my name. For signs that I deserved it, and the love that ricocheted between my father, his mother and me. Certainly I closely watched Kristina for clues, about what the name implied for me, what I had inherited in its sing-song rhythm. But it was difficult: my grandmother was a widow by then and entirely set in the ways of living alone. And there was this other thing: despite the name and all the magic I'd applied to it, I saw that we might not share many qualities, that we had very different temperaments. We were different people, she and I.

The word that came immediately to my mind about Kristina was *formidable.* Her willowy frame and jet-black hair added to a demeanour that suggested, immediately, that Farmor did things her own way and wouldn't brook any argument. The menu at her cottage gave us an early lesson. Nothing was wasted; not the crumbs from the table, swept into her cupped hand and tipped into the mortar and pestle; not teabags, which were used three times before they were reluctantly discarded.

And worse: solidified leftovers from breakfast porridge were later fried in butter like a pancake and served up for lunch. My younger brothers found this meal inedible—I didn't like it much either—and Farmor was displeased. When my father defended his sons, she stalked away with her head in the air, refusing to speak to anyone for hours. The boys, meanwhile, flew down to the village square for *korv*, the tasty Swedish hotdogs that reminded them of home. I was torn between distaste and needing her approval. But my mother was unequivocal: *don't eat it if you don't like it.* The recycled porridge wasn't offered to us again.

SHE SAYS, *I was mean to Wawa today.* We're visiting Zoza—my daughter, Zoe—during her lunch break. Zoza hears the confession as she clips Amber into her car seat after our Thursday ice-cream. Both faces turn towards me, but before I can confirm it she puts her hand to Zoe's cheek. *I said sorry*, she says.

I PLANNED AND SAVED HARD to go back to Sweden after that first trip, but university got in the way and my grandmother died before I could make it. She had wanted me to have her old piano, my father told me, but he doubted it would survive the journey by sea. In its place I have two spoons, a cake knife inscribed *KO*, an unfinished piece of embroidery framed on my wall, some hand-sewn table-runners of the kind common in all Swedish houses. And a recipe book, *Hemmets Kokbok*, in which Farmor left small scraps of writing: shopping lists, a menu, a variation of ingredients. Against some she has written the year and the varied amounts—1960, *en kopp socker*, 1961, 10 *lit. vatten*—experimenting with sugar and water in the salted ham. Against another, *Norska kransar* (roughly, Norwegian plaited bread), she has simply written *mycket god*. Very good.

I examine these things closely. In the fine stitching, the knife's smooth handle, the writing, I suppose I am once more looking for signs and clues, to erase the years with my hand laid over the shadow of hers. In the end, though, I have to admit defeat: as a grandmother, Kristina remains a long way away; her thoughts and the ways of her heart are still mysteries to me.

But these things that have been bequeathed to me make me look hard at the objects in my own home. Years from now, will a spoon, a teapot, a bookmark be transformed in the hands of my grand-daughter simply because they were mine? I'd like to think they might contain something magic within them for her. The spoon or bookmark as talisman perhaps, something that will insist on continuity, on remembrance.

But then, I remind myself, these are just objects. Real continuity isn't found there; it's found in looks and habits, movements inherited and learned. I'd like to think it will happen like this: one day, she will catch herself pursing her lips in a particular way, or hear herself uttering a familiar phrase, or see, as she raises a glass or a cup, the shape of her fingernails, and think, *they are hers.* I would like to think she will smile, recognising us both.

IF IT'S RAINING she organises rugs and pillows inside and says, *I'll be the mummy and you be the darling.* She reads to me from an upside-down book in a schoolmarmish way, looking up occasionally to instruct me: *Don't open your eyes, my darling. Hold the teddy tight. Don't smile!*

One night, I watch as she and her father read the same story to each other on the sofa. They are tucked together like spoons, both more than tired. It's past their bedtimes. In a pause in the reading she turns to him and reaches to place one palm against his cheek. Then the other against the other cheek. *Dano*, she says, quietly, tenderly, *when are you going to marry me?*

I HAVE A PHOTOGRAPH of my mother with a baby grandson taken when Drew was four or five months old. I love this photo: they are both laughing at someone or something outside the camera frame, big spontaneous belly-laughs that stretch their mouths and light their eyes. He is a beautiful baby and this is a rare picture of my mother laughing, really laughing. But this isn't why I love it, or not exactly. It's the timing. The laugh has burst from them both at the same split-second, as if they are not quite separate, as if they are joined, grafted together at some point, old skin and new.

I drew upon this photo for inspiration in one of my novels, *The China Garden*, giving it to a grandmother character who, I realise as I write this, is loved by her grandchild in just the way I want to be loved by mine. This isn't because she is a perfect grandmother—she is as flawed and frail as the rest of us—or because she has extraordinary skills. In the novel Kieran loves his grandmother Cress, thoughtlessly and unconditionally, for the opposite reasons. It is, I think, because she has always been there, as if she is a part of him, a part of his own ordinary life. To him, Cress is 'elemental, like his hands and feet, daily, precious, unregarded'.

Cress—guilt-ridden, pining for her lost faith, a kleptomaniac—is not my mother, nor based upon her. Though my mother had her own guilt, her own losses—a baby son, snatched from her arms, stolen by her violent Greek husband in the days when such things were played down, not quite condoned but shrugged off. She didn't see her son again for thirty-seven years. I'm not sure if, like Cress, she also lost her religion after that, but she certainly lost her faith in the world. It was a world complicit in her tragedy. She vigilantly watched the rest of her children—those of us born in happier times to a gentler man—for any signs they too might be lost, by her hand or by our own; precarious hobbies we pursued, dangerous lovers, an oversupply of trust or arrogance or melancholy. All these unsettled her—she became anxious, controlling. But with her grandchildren, she was different.

From the birth of the first one, she seemed to lose her fear. It was replaced with something more sinuous, more determined and quiet, as if she had begun at last to believe in her own power. Or perhaps her own goodness. Her sense of that had disappeared with her stolen son—how could a *good* woman lose a child? A good woman would have somehow prevented it, no matter how big and brutal the thief. I know she thought this because, reflecting upon the mistakes I have made with my own children, I have at times believed myself bad too. Marked.

But my mother's new, better self emerged as she inserted herself—effortlessly, seamlessly—into her grandchildren's lives. She came into being with her name: *Mimi*. I saw it as she walked the babies around the garden, naming flowers, as she taught her grandsons how to knit, as she convinced her grand-daughters how *beautiful* they were, how courageous, how clever. Urged them to be *tenacious* in the face of fear, difficult arithmetic, wayward needles and thread. Told her grandsons that they would never, ever fight a war that wasn't theirs. It was a decree: no more lost boys.

ANNA, the director of the kindy she goes to three times a week, is Danish and so also a *Farmor.* She spends considerable time trying to coax the proper word from

Amber, who resists, glancing at Anna as if she has two heads. *Say Farmor,* Anna urges when I arrive at the end of the day to pick her up. Amber sighs. *Farmor,* she obliges, not looking at me. We go inside to collect her bag and as we leave Amber makes a detour in Anna's direction. She plants two feet—in glittery fairy shoes—firmly in front of her and waggles her finger. *You can't call her Farmor,* she says, her eyes stern. *She's Wawa.* Then she spins around, waves goodbye to her friends. We race each other to the car.

NAMES AND NAMING have long been fascinations for me. I'm intrigued by the way naming bestows meaning, its potential for magic. But since Amber arrived I contemplate it more and more. Lately, I have begun to understand that the process of giving a child a name, and with it a shape to step into, can also work in reverse. Amber is not named for anyone in the family, but she has named me, and in so doing brought a different 'me' into being. Just as my mother was re-born as Mimi, so I have become, through Amber, a new and enlarged version of myself.

With Wawa, Amber has created a shape for me to step into, a role to fill. It is a shape both familiar and strange to me: it recalls, I think, different aspects of the child I was, the woman I became before the world intervened. I try to renew it every day, try to keep up—with this grandmother, me, and the daily shaping and re-shaping of Amber herself, every new facet she reveals.

Perhaps, I think now, this is the magic that grandparents are imbued with, this shape-shifting: the ability to be reliable and ordinary, part of a daily or weekly landscape, as unremarkable as a tree or a bug, and as enchanting.

SHE'S WRAPPING HER BEAR in a tea towel when her grandfather plumps down beside her. *I've just got one thing to say to you, Amber Jean*, he says. Her eyes don't stray from her task. *What?* she says. She's concentrating on the folds. The tea towel is too short.

I think you are a very, very beautiful girl.

She lowers the bear then and looks up, cocking her head at him, considering. Then, deadpan, she says, *Thank you so, so much, Tony Macaroni. Thank you for being so, so kind to me.*

That's okay, he shrugs, watching as she continues with the wrapping and patting. Then she glances up again, leans towards him, plants a loud kiss on his lips. *And thank you for loving me so, so much.* She turns away to tuck the bear into bed.

WHERE DO WE LOOK to find our own ways of being a grandmother, to be with this child of our child? Although the grandmother of my novel is a fiction, I can see that she and my mother shared a gift for grandmothering, habits and ways that I have carried around in my old string bag of memory, waiting beneath all the shinier, newer habits I've tried out. But it was fictional Cress, and the ties she has with Kieran, who showed me the way.

Cress showed me that my mother's magic was ordinary magic. Quietly, unspectacularly, just like Cress, my mother made herself part of her grandchildren's ordinary lives—daily, precious, largely unregarded. She was just Mimi, always there, her love for them plain but visceral—it was a bodily love that encompassed the smell of their skin and the shape of their hands, the curve of their hips, along with the flash of a spirit, a character she identified early in each one. My mother's heart was on her sleeve, her love uncontested. Her goodness was tangible, visible. It drew her grandchildren to her like moths to a flame.

This, I know now, might be the greatest gift of grandmothering—of grandfathering too, if men allow it, or choose it. I can see that with Amber, I too have stopped being afraid. I have begun to believe again in my own goodness. To allow all my mistakes and inadequacies as a mother to not so much dissipate—I can't deny them—but to be forgiven, made up for, alchemised by this child of my child. In this way Amber herself may be the magician.

THE FIRST WORDS she learned to sing were *somewhere, over the rainbow*, her voice rising on the first syllable of *rainbow* and her lips pursed severely over the second. On the swing at the park down the hill, she throws back her head and sings it to the sky. When we stop swinging and climbing and butterfly hunting, she sits opposite me on the picnic bench with her cheese sandwich raised and says, *So, Wawa, how was your day?*

At sunset, we find Eeyore, her bear, the flowers and weeds she's gathered for her mother, and trail reluctantly towards home. As we climb the hill she sweeps her arm towards the pastel horizon. *Oh look!* she says in a stage whisper, urgent. *There they are! My favourite, favourite pink clouds.* She instructs Eeyore to look too, holding him high so his glassy eyes might see.

An hour later, she falls asleep to a slowed-down version of *Old MacDonald*. I make the *eeyi eeyi oh* into a steady, mournful dirge. It works every time. She slumps in my arms and I hold her, the sweet apple smell of her breath on my face. Surely, I think, this is the best it can be, the best *I* can be. The dark comes and still I sit with her, unwilling to relinquish who I am here. Named, chosen.

The End of the Line

ANNETTE SHUN WAH

IT WAS A STIFLINGLY HOT DAY when the family moved into their new home, so they carried the old woman in first, to get her out of the searing heat. With the heat came the flies, and the old matriarch was in no mood for them. As she tried in vain to swat her persistent black tormentors, she cursed them shrilly: 'I wish each of you would drop dead as you come through the door!' In the ensuing months, tragedy struck. One by one, the family members succumbed to illness or mishap. The order in which they perished coincided with the order in which each had entered their new house that fateful day. The old woman had forgotten that the first words uttered in a new home became prophecy. Her curse, intended for the flies, had instead befallen her loved ones.

This was my father's favourite boyhood story, and I am reminded of it whenever I think about my paternal grandmother, Yau Sam Moy. Not that she put any curses on us exactly, but she had a mysterious power over us all.

Grandma would live with us for a few months at a time, then move on to another of my father's siblings. Townsville, Wollongong and Brisbane—a relentless circuit for a frail old lady who, surely, should have simply settled down to dote in her old age. While the cousins of my generation thought of it as sharing our grandmother around, and our parents regarded it as sharing the load of caring for her, my grandmother was well past polite notions about sharing. Like a spider she was weaving a web, round and round, closely, carefully, tightly—not to catch anything but to cocoon everything that she held precious.

Having Grandma come to stay wasn't like having any other houseguest. Her mere presence seemed to upset the natural order. My father was still the head of the household, but somehow everyone seemed to move down a rung. It didn't matter much to me because being the youngest, I was used to being at the bottom of the pecking order. But my stepmother didn't take quite so kindly to it.

My grandmother and my father sometimes spoke to each other in a language no one else could understand. It was a language called *hakka*. The rest of us spoke normal, garden variety Cantonese. English was banished from the home, partly out of respect for my stepmother who couldn't speak it, but also because my father believed it was crucial for us to remain as Chinese as possible. Neither of my brothers learnt English until they went to school, but they must have flaunted the 'no *faan wa* (foreign language) at home' rule, because by the time I came along, I could jabber away in both languages. *Hakka* was a special kind of Chinese that even my mother didn't understand. 'We're *hakka* people,' my father would proudly proclaim.

As if it wasn't confusing enough being Chinese and Cantonese as well, even though my brother Doug and I were both born in Australia. It was only the eldest, Tom, who'd been born in China. Come to think of it, my father and all his brothers and sisters were born in Australia and so too, was my grandmother. Did this make Tom the most Chinese of all of us? This *hakka* thing just muddied up the picture even more. But asking questions didn't help. No one had the time to explain anything to me. I was expected to just accept whatever I was told.

I don't think my stepmother liked it when her husband and mother-in-law broke into their strange dialect. It was like they were talking about her behind her back, but right in front of her face! She'd get her own back at night, when she and Dad were in their bedroom behind closed doors, and the hisses of their whispered arguments would slither down the hallway to my room where Grandma slept in my bed while I wriggled my bony body between the wires of the camp stretcher. If she heard any of the commotion she'd never let on. She'd just reposition herself to get more comfortable, and soon her snores would cancel out whatever sibilance still waited in the hall.

Grandma wore loose cotton dresses and sensible shoes, and moved more slowly than everyone else. We had to treat her with the utmost respect, because she was easily offended by our boisterous young ways. I spent more time than anyone with Grandma during her visits. My brothers went to school, and my parents went to work, and she would stay home to look after me. Although it sometimes seemed more like I was looking after her. Grandma didn't take me on outings to the zoo, nor did she read me fairytales or bake special sweet treats like other children's grandmothers. We would stay home, and I'd do her bidding, kneading her broad shoulders to squeeze out the stiffness of old age, thumping out the aches from her forehead, making little kung fu chops up and down her restless legs, or squeezing the blackheads on the bridge of her nose.

While we were busily tiptoeing around, shovelling on the reverence and consideration that her position and age required of us, it was easy to forget some very important things about her. This was a woman who had brought up seven children and run a family business in the middle of nowhere. The fragility of old age concealed a pluckiness well beyond our juvenile perceptions of what old people were capable of. I suppose it never occurred to me that she'd ever been anything but old and slow, too timid to venture far from home. I couldn't have been more wrong.

Yau Sam Moy was born in Palmerston, later to become Darwin, in Australia's Top End in 1892. The official records will tell you there were only about a dozen Chinese women in the Northern Territory at the time—including Grandma, her two older sisters and their mother. Like her sisters, she was married at eighteen to a suitor chosen by their mother. Great-grandmother had extraordinary connections. Even from the remoteness of Darwin in the early 1900s she was able to track down an eligible Chinese merchant from the same tribe—a *hakka* man from Hong Kong. By marrying him, Grandma surrendered her Australian-born British status to a man who'd very likely entered the country illegally. That's just the way things were done back then.

I've been told two things about my grandfather, Ju Yor Kee: he liked to start every day with a whisky, and he was dead by the time my grandmother turned thirty-five. They'd left Darwin in 1910—joining the exodus of Chinese ahead of the Federal Government taking over administration of the Northern Territory. The Chinese had been instrumental in establishing a settlement in the Top End. Three previous attempts to do so had failed miserably in the remote and harsh conditions. Only with the perseverance of the Chinese was a town eventually established and developed into a thriving community. But there was something wrong with this picture—at least in the eyes of the powerbrokers from the southern capitals. Australia was for the white man, and the white man was overwhelmingly outnumbered in the Territory by the Aborigines and the 'Asiatics' as they were referred to in polite company. So it was a case of 'Thanks for the hard work, for putting up with the isolation, the monsoons, the malaria and the cyclones, but now that you've built a bustling little town you can drop everything and just move along'. New rules made it virtually impossible for most Chinese to continue to make a living, and those who could afford it went back to China, including my great-grandmother, who dug up her husband's bones and took him home. But my grandparents were just starting out. There wasn't much of a future back in the ancestral village for them, or the children they were duty bound to have. They would have to seek out new opportunities somewhere in Australia.

The newlyweds set off for Longreach, a marathon journey by steamboat around Cape York and halfway down the Queensland coastline to Rockhampton where one of Grandma's sisters had settled. But that was just a pit stop. They boarded the train and headed west as far as it could go. There are always opportunities at the end of the line, and the end of this line was Longreach, a remote town surrounded by extensive cattle stations. That's where my grandparents set up shop—a general store in the main street.

Seven children later, and grandfather was dead. Not from having the children, mind you. That didn't really take much effort on his part. And not from the whisky either, but from typhoid—a common visitor to a town that kept the dust down by dampening its dirt roads with liquid from the dunny collection.

So how does a Chinese woman cope in 1920s Queensland, widowed with seven children? I don't know about any other woman, but Grandma, without any formal schooling or social networks to speak of and barely tall enough to reach the top shelf, coped marvellously. It's as if her husband's death mattered little more than the passing of a cloud, and indeed she'd later remark to one of her daughters-in-law that he'd been so useless, if she ever returned to Longreach she'd 'turn him over in his grave'!

Grandma not only ran the general store, but developed several sidelines. She'd get up at three o'clock every morning to fire up the stove and bake meat pies. They did a particularly good trade on a Saturday, when she loaded up huge baskets of hot crusty pies for her sons to carry to the local cinema to sell at interval. Can you believe that? My Chinese granny pioneering the meat pie business in Longreach. Even today the old-timers up there don't remember much about the family, but they do remember the pies—the best they'd ever tasted before or since. I'd hazard a guess there was a dash of soy sauce in the gravy.

But there was more. Grandma grew up in a traditional Chinese household that did not send its girls to school. Yet she developed her handwriting skills by icing the fancy cakes she made for the town's wedding and birthday celebrations. Her copperplate signature shines firm and resolute amidst the messy bureaucratic scrawl on the family's many official documents.

No wonder her shoulders used to ache and her legs were restless. All that making and baking, standing for hours on the ungiving kitchen floor, the oven like a furnace in the height of an outback Queensland summer. She was made of strong stuff, the stuff of pioneering women.

There were many who didn't see that toughness. They saw only what they wanted to see: a tiny Chinese woman struggling on her own, ripe for the plucking. They tried it on. Of course they did. Like the man who bought a wagonload of goods and never paid her for them; or the lodger who skipped out on months of rent. Did I tell you that she'd accumulated enough money to own several properties around town? Yet another con man tried to talk his way out of paying for purchases. None of them got away with it. It's all there in the town's police records. She took them to court, and she won every case.

But there were things that did defeat her. I learnt about one from another of my father's favourite stories, which is what had sent me off to search through those court records. My older uncles, young men by then, had gotten into a fight with some of the locals. My father supposed it was about the same old thing that all the fights of his boyhood had been about—racist taunts. You see, according to him, theirs was the only Chinese family in town. Sure there were other Chinese men, many single, some married to non-Chinese women, but a Chinese family was rare in Longreach in the 1910s and 1920s and there was a price to pay for being different. It wasn't so much a fight as an all-out brawl. Police were called and charges laid, but when the circuit judge came to town my uncles dressed for the hearing in schoolboy shorts and long socks. With their slicked-down hair and smooth hairless faces, they looked ten years younger than they actually were. The judge took one look at them and threw the case out of court, berating his officers for charging these 'children' and advised their opponents that they'd better stick to picking on someone their own age! I'd like to think the town's Chinese laughed about that one all the way back to China.

But pulling the wool over the judge's eyes was a hollow victory. Not long after this, Grandma made a momentous decision. She sold up all her properties, packed up the shop and took the family 'back' to China. She wanted her children to learn about their Chinese culture, to be among others who cherished their Chineseness rather than despised for it. And so, on Foundation Day 1932, Grandma and her seven little Australians boarded the SS *Changte* for the gut-churning voyage across ominous seas back to the land of their ancestors.

According to tradition, when a woman marries she becomes a part of her husband's family, and forsakes her own. And so, Grandma had been dutifully sending funds 'home'—that is to her husband's ancestral village—for decades, carefully scrimping whatever she could so as to send a respectable token of her filial piety. Still the urgent requests came from her husband's brother and his bossy wife—send more. Repairs were needed, extensions for the growing family, unexpected expenses. She complied, of course, and now she felt it was time to take her offspring there, to be part of an extended family for the first time in their lives.

But repairs had not been carried out. Extensions had not been constructed. Not so much as a coat of paint had been attempted. The place was looking decidedly shabby compared with the fine buildings on the main street of Longreach. To add insult to injury, Grandma and her children were received not as honoured guests, but as little more than servants in the feudal household, having to waiting their turn for leftovers from the dinner table. All that money she had sent faithfully over the years had gone up in her brother-in-law's opium pipe. If she'd been expecting any gratitude, that had turned to smoke long ago.

Grandma had made a terrible mistake, uprooted her family and travelled all this way, for a slap in the face. But she had come to China for a reason, and she was not to be beaten so easily. Against daunting odds, she struck out on her own, eventually establishing a base in Hong Kong. There was no one to guide her but equally, no one to stand in her way—no husband to placate, no mother-in-law to obey, even her own mother and sisters were scattered far and wide and had long ago stopped telling

Sam Moy what she should do. She truly was the matriarch of this family.

So Hong Kong is where they settled, and my grandmother sat back to watch as her children married and began the next generation. Just as it seemed she had found a place to call home, the events of World War II and the Communist uprising forced the family to flee once again, this time scattering them all over China. Only after the war did they regroup in Hong Kong, Grandma reeling them in like a skilled fly fisherman. Eventually, all bar one of the family returned to Australia, the land of their birth, safe from the political uncertainties of the new China. Until her final days Grandma would not settle. Moving from son to daughter to son, she tightened her hold on the family, desperate to guide their destinies to the very end.

I was only six years old when my grandmother died, felled by a stroke. Only then, when my father and his siblings gathered to bury her in Townsville, were they able to shake free of her strange power. Her funeral brought them together one last time, but then, like ships that have slipped their moorings our families drifted into storms of our own making.

Unlike the old woman in my father's story there are no curses cast by my grandmother. She was fiercely independent and resourceful, headstrong and resilient, formidable and courageous, a survivor, and that remains her legacy.

This Dearest Freshness

GABRIELLE LORD

'WOULD YOU RATHER BE Nanna or Grandma?' my daughter asked.

For a few seconds I was puzzled, then I got it. Madeleine was announcing her pregnancy to me—in terms of the relationship *I* would have with the unborn baby. In those moments, a split-second pang of loss hit me; a strange, sad feeling. Later, I realised what it was: the coming baby would be her closest relative. My time occupying that position was over.

At that stage, ten years ago, I didn't want to take either name, deciding instead to wait until after the birth. Maybe the 'right' name would emerge. This proved to be the case.

Later on in her pregnancy, Madeleine asked me if I would be a birth attendant, together with her husband.

And I was very happy, if somewhat apprehensive, to accept her offer.

DURING THE MONTHS of my daughter's first pregnancy, my own mother was dying. Nursed by my father, a retired general practitioner, my mother was able to stay in her own bedroom in her own house right up until the very last few days. My time in those months seemed to be spread between ferrying chicken soup and foot massages to my mother and driving up to my daughter, to give her lots of body massages—partly for her pleasure and well-being, but also because I hoped the baby would get used to my voice and my touch even before the birth. I was already becoming a grandmother.

The call came early on the morning of the twenty-fourth of January and I set out to drive from Clovelly to Mona Vale birthing centre. My mood was one of apprehension, excitement and that unique sense of approaching an experience for the very first time.

Imagine my astonishment and shock when at the top of York Street in Randwick, near the bus depot, I saw four black horses, funereal plumes floating from their foreheads, trotting in the opposite lane, drawing a gleaming black Victorian coach hearse! I continued my drive, wondering if I'd somehow stumbled into a parallel universe. Had I hallucinated the whole episode? Was it some kind of dark epiphany, reminding me that as new life comes into the world, another life leaves?

It was a long day. Made longer by my daughter's misunderstanding of the midwife's instruction to push *harder*, when what was intended was an instruction to *sustain* the pushes longer. Finally came the awful moment when Madeleine's despairing and anguished blue eyes beseeched me: 'Mum, I just can't do this. I can't push any harder. I can't do it.'

She was exhausted. I felt despairing. There was nothing I could do to help my daughter. The doctor was outside sharpening his scalpel. It seemed that an episiotomy was unavoidable.

However, in the nick of time, the midwife explained herself better and Cassie was born quite quickly after that, distressed and having inhaled meconium. The poor little baby was handled quite roughly as the meconium was sucked from her windpipe, the vitamin K injection was whacked into her tiny thigh, and she was weighed in like a jockey and his saddle after a race. She had suffered a lot. However, minutes later, she was being comforted on her mother's breast—the great teaching of this moment: life can be very difficult, baby, often a painful struggle, *but comfort can be found*.

Postnatal difficulties meant that my daughter had to be wheeled away to the operating theatre for an hour and a half. While she was being attended to I held the new baby, my grand-daughter. In that time, it happened. As I bonded with her, she became my baby too. Later, with Cassie safely on her mother's breast, when I went to the bathroom, I found blood on my pants.

UNTIL CASSIE ARRIVED, I don't think I truly understood what unconditional love really felt like. I knew it as an intellectual concept—that one cares for another person without any desire for any particular form of reciprocity. But this was *experiential*—like falling in love, an overwhelming, embodied *surge*; an outpouring of my heart, body and soul, flowing into the life of another being.

I drove up to the northern side of the city every few days—I had to see her, be with her. My Greek neighbour used to say about her new grand-daughter: 'My heart aches when I don't see her.'

My daughter and I quickly learned Cassie's repertoire of non-verbal language. One day the two of us were down the street when my son-in-law, who was minding Cassie, rang.

'I think the baby is having an asthma attack,' he said. 'She's doing this funny breathing.'

My daughter and I looked at each other. 'Warm up a bottle for her, darling,' said my daughter. 'That's just her milky noise.'

I felt sad for my son-in-law that the circumstances of his life and his career meant he hadn't had a chance to learn his baby daughter's language.

From the time Cassie was only a few months old, I would steal her away for weekends together, waking up to her rounded cheek and dark eyelashes half turned away on the pillow, her body a small, very warm and damp caterpillar next to me. As she grew older and could toddle, I'd sit with her at the beach down the street, watching her turn shells over, or examine sand and seaweed, or simply studying grass; noticing the angled shape of the blades and the tiny hairs on one side, was deeply satisfying for both of us. Her discovery of the world brought a fresh vividness to every experience. Even before she could say many words, the question in her eyes when she looked to me for an answer after noticing a dead fruit bat swinging on the telegraph wires required my response.

'He's dead,' I said. 'Poor old fruit bat was killed by the electricity in the wires.'

Some months later when we were at a holiday house, Cassie was standing on a stool beside the stove while I stirred the porridge. She was puzzled at the glowing hotplate, quite different from the gas flame at home. Another questioning gaze.

'It's an electric stove,' I said. 'Electricity makes it hot.'

She drew back immediately. I could see she was troubled.

'Are you thinking of that fruit bat?' I asked.

Slowly, solemnly, she nodded.

When she was about fifteen months old, I took Cassie to the old Manly Vale Montessori playgroup twice a week, driving up from Clovelly, picking her up from home, then spending the next couple of hours with her at the under-three playgroup where she applied herself to the serious business of painting, making waterwheels spin, preparing snacks of cheese and apple for us, opening various sorts of latches and handles, measuring water out into jugs and cups, washing up her snack plates, walking along planks, climbing on ropes and monkey bars. Later, I'd try to get her to have a nap in the car, driving around for ages. But she rarely slept more than about twenty to thirty minutes during the day. It was as if she was scared of missing out on too much.

When she was three, she started attending the Montessori kindergarten and later, the extended day care. When I was with her, I completely gave myself over to the experience. Unlike her parents, who were busy with their everyday responsibilities of getting to work, making meals, always busy with housework or shopping, I could just *be* with her. That is the gift grandmothers and grandfathers can bring. We don't have the responsibilities of parenting anymore.

CASSIE WAS AT THE just-beginning-to-talk stage—'Ma-ma', 'Dad-da' and 'Bub-ba'—when she began to call me '*Yia-Yia*', the Greek diminutive for 'Nanna'. I wondered if some strange karmic force was at work—my great-grandfather, Konstantinos Kougousakis, had come to Australia from Crete. In any case, Yia-Yia I have remained—for all the family.

Occasionally, Cassie had her two-year-old tantrums and had to be sent to her room for 'time out'. She would beat on the door, calling out for Mummy, then Daddy. And when neither of those people came, she'd start calling for me.

'Yia-Yia,' she'd cry.

My heart would be torn. It took everything I had to remain calm and respectful of her parents' decision not to open the door until the storm had at least started to subside. Every fibre of my being wanted to race into that room, grab her up and run away with her!

I once read of a grandmother who'd fought with a crocodile until it released her grand-daughter. Now I understood that fierce, protective and overwhelming love. It was stronger than the love I'd had for my daughter—at nineteen I was pretty emotionally thin and as a mother I had expectations of how my daughter 'should be'. It's sad that the maturity needed so much in raising children, rarely comes to us until we're too old to be doing it.

As my grand-daughter grew I witnessed her developing mind seeing connections, noticing similarities and differences, making comparisons: 'Puffballs are like the fireworks,' she observed, around age three, blowing dandelion seed heads away. And another time: 'Dragonflies are like little helicopters,' as she watched one hover on the spot in her garden.

When Cassie was about two and a half, her sister Georgia arrived in the world, born before I could get there. By the time I arrived, she was already sleeping in her bassinet. She'd arrived in about three and a half hours. Despite my son-in-law ringing several times, I'd failed to hear the phone through a night of very heavy rain.

This time, there were no Victorian hearses, no medical emergency, no need for me to hold the new baby for an hour and a half. The bonding did not happen then. My relationship with my second grand-daughter started out very differently.

The second baby has to fit into the space already very much taken up by three people—her mother, father and older sister. The second baby (especially one of the same gender) has to grow up with a sibling who will always be just that much ahead of her—someone who will always know more, be stronger, seem smarter, taller and more competent. Georgia responded by adopting and developing areas that were her very own. She became the artistic one, the athletic one, the imaginative, dreamy one. Fairy La-la. She became the clown. She also learned how to deal with her older sister.

'Just because you're very smart, Cassie, it doesn't mean you're perfect.'

As they both grow (Cassie is now eleven, and Georgia now eight) I feel I've missed out somewhat on Georgia. The last two years have been very busy for me, professionally speaking, and I haven't had the same amount of free time available to do as many of those important grand-mothering things, such as looking at the angled blades of grass. Another writer once described to me how she and her grand-daughter played, passing a packet of pasta backwards and forwards repeatedly from a cupboard, and the intense pleasure this simple activity delivered. These games—the grass-watching and the pasta-passing—bring intense satisfaction because of their depth and meditative focus. Witnessing the development of a human being, sharing the new human's zest and enthusiasm for this amazing world is a powerfully intriguing pastime, 'There lives the dearest freshness deep down things,' Gerard Manley Hopkins reminds us and the new, shining eyes of a baby help us older women find this dearest freshness all over again.

Sometimes I sit cross-legged on the floor with Georgia. We make necklaces and we play cat's cradle. One afternoon, when Georgie was seven, we produced the whole of the *Sleeping Beauty* ballet complete with Tchaikovsky's music, using tiny paper figures and a little stage. As we packed it away, she looked up and said, 'You're a very nice Yia-Yia.' It warmed my heart. It's always good to be acknowledged!

I've also been fortunate enough to have an extra pair of grand-daughters (who also call me Yia-Yia), the twins from my son-in-law's first marriage, with whom I have a growing relationship. I didn't see them a great deal when they were smaller, however in the last few years, with the girls in their teens, I've come to love and admire them. Holly and Amber not only bring benign and loving older sister energy to their younger sisters, but their dignity and beauty, their straight-out *goodness* of heart, and their affectionate natures enhance the family.

How different then is my own experience of my grandmothers. My paternal grandmother was a tall, distant and benevolent presence. Ma, who'd fallen in love with a handsome Irishman she'd seen on the tram and wrangled an introduction to, lived with my grandfather in one of the four houses given her as a marriage gift by her father, because she'd 'married a man on a wage'. My grandfather was a draftsman for the old GPO, and that was certainly not considered grand enough for the eldest Miss Foley, daughter of Bartholomew Foley, Esq., wealthy merchant of Sydney. Her three sisters did not attend the wedding and remained unreconciled for over a decade.

Ma raised four children, born during and after the 'Great War', my father being the second. My youngest uncle lived with her, remaining a bachelor—and in that house—to the end of his days. Together with my father and my younger brother—while my mother stayed home with the very young ones and the latest baby (there are six of us)—I visited Ma and Pa at regular intervals. Once Ma helped me with making a dress for a doll. Another time, she shaped my fingernails into little pointed 'roofs' and later, when I was eleven and being 'confirmed', she was my sponsor, giving me a beautiful crystal rosary and rosary bracelet as a Confirmation gift. Some years later, when I married, her words to me were, 'I hope you'll be as happy as Ferdie and I were. We never had an angry word.' That's one way of (not) dealing with conflict.

When Ma died, I was twenty-eight with a nine-year-old daughter, doing a full-time Honours year at university. I heard she'd left me a diamond ring and I knew exactly which ring it was—her 'Sunday ring', an eternity ring, given to her by her 'man on a wage' husband and which at first she only used to wear to mass on Sundays. Once or twice, when I discovered her wearing it on weekdays, I scolded her. Obviously Ma remembered that. When I wear that ring today—and I wear it every day—I think of her with fondness and regret all the world of things I don't know about her, like what it was like to be shunned by one's sisters, to marry against the family's wishes.

MY MOTHER'S MOTHER is an even more shadowy presence in my mind. Unlike my memory of Ma, I have no image of Nanna's face. But even as a small child I sensed a sad and quietly agitated woman. She lived with us for a time when I was five or so and I remember her Eno's Salts which she took every morning to help her dyspepsia. My mother used to boast what intelligent children she had, because we never ran outside onto the busy road in front of our house. She had no idea that Nanna had told us that if we ever were to do this, old 'Diggly Bones' would get us and put us in his bag; she even pointed him out to us, an old man we'd see working at the convent across the road, a heavy sack over his shoulders. She'd constantly remind us, 'Don't put that penny in your mouth. It might have been in an old Chinaman's sock.' And she cooked Frizzled Dick—bread fried in bacon fat and salt.

Thanks to a second cousin, I have an oval, sepia portrait of Nanna as a young woman—Marcel waves and fox furs surrounding a sweet, 1920s face. The only words I recall ever saying to her were: 'I'll never be a boarder at boarding school.' When she died I was six and away at boarding school, so I only found out about her death some time later, after the funeral.

MY OWN MOTHER was ambivalent about grandmothering. She was a correct rather than close grandmother to both my and my siblings' children. We could visit with our kids and have cups of tea and cakes with her, the grandchildren might play the piano for her or perform in some way, and they were always included in Easter and Christmas gatherings at my parents' place. But apart from occasional outings—pantomimes, the ballet, or other such treats—she was not interested in fostering close relationships. This was consistent with her nature—she was not a person to whom intimacy came easily. (It took me many years of painful psychotherapy and growth to change this sad deficiency in myself so as not to pass it on to yet another generation.)

My husband's mother, on the other hand, was a very warm and loving grandma. We often stayed with her and Harry at the Kurrajong orchard, and Danma (my daughter's early attempt at 'Grandma') would set a special little breakfast table for Madeleine, so that it was always ready when she woke up. Harry sometimes took her up with him on the tractor, when slashing weeds between the rows of trees. At a time when Madeleine's own mother (me!) was young and restless and incapable of deep mothering, Danma provided complete and unconditional attention to that little girl, a gift that I believe has contributed hugely to the sweetness and steadiness of my daughter's nature. I owe my mother-in-law a huge debt. But I was unaware of that—among other things—when I ran away from her son, my husband, taking her only grandchild, my eight-year-old daughter, with me. Angry and hurt, I wanted nothing more to do with my husband—including his family. It never occurred to me that by leaving him, I had also 'divorced' a loving grandmother—and grandfather—from their grand-daughter. Knowing little of loving relationships in those days, I remained unaware of the pain I was causing, and those two people suffered greatly from their separation from a grand-daughter they loved dearly.

IN AUGUST 2008, a group of British grandparents moved towards creating a charter of grandparents' rights. This was not so much about visiting rights or access rights, but more about protecting themselves from being overly used as unpaid childminders by their thoughtless adult children. These grandparents were complaining about long hours of travelling to pick their grandchildren up and long hours spent minding them. (More often than not, 'grandparents' means 'grandmother'. Minding children still tends to be women's work.)

The words 'minding' and 'baby *sitting*' seem part of a conspiracy to conceal the reality of what it takes to care for children. These expressions make it sound easy and unskilled—and *relaxing.* (Why would you want to pay people who are having *such a holiday*?) These words imply that all one has to do is lounge around, relaxing at the beach or on the couch, reading a book, while the babies and young children quietly tumble happily around amusing themselves. Anyone who has had anything to do with young children knows that child minding is *a constant and focused responsibility*, taking lots of energy and intelligence. Having babies is a young woman's game—and for good reason. Nature reduces fertility quite quickly, as many women in their thirties, and sometimes forties, regretfully discover. And older women, in their fifties, sixties and seventies, simply don't have the energy and physical resources to cope for long hours without respite from the relentless demands of small children.

This was brought home to me in a very personal way some years back when I looked after Georgie for ten days while her sister and parents were away. Being alone for twenty-four hours a day, day after day, with a two-and-a-half-year-old who had just seen everyone else in her family disappearing in a car, proved extremely difficult. The little one would not let me out of her sight, even standing beside me when I was in the toilet!

I was on the go with her from six o'clock in the morning—'Up! Yia-Yia! Up!'—to around seven or eight o'clock at night. By the fifth day, I was surprised to find myself in tears. And it wasn't because Georgie was difficult or demanding. On the contrary. But she was two and a half, which meant that I had to be in constant attendance, relieved only for those few minutes when she might draw a picture or eat a meal. On the sixth day, I invited myself over to my sister's place, so as not to be so alone, and to be where there were other older children for Georgie to interact with, at least in the evenings and early mornings. I had forgotten what it was like to be an isolated mother.

No doubt grandmothers feel guilty when they find they *can't* do it—or at least not for extended lengths of time. After all, grandchildren are our flesh and blood and, in most cases, greatly loved. I imagine some people might become resentful because they feel they can't say no to their adult children's requests. But it's not as if grandmothers have nothing else to do. Like many others, I have an extremely busy professional and private life.

I only 'do' a couple of days with the grandchildren every school holidays, and although I find it tiring, I wouldn't miss it for anything. Each time I see my grand-daughters I can't believe how quickly the time has passed since that first baby lay on the pillow next to me. She has grown into a self-possessed eleven-year-old who has lots of friends, goes away with the school to camp in the bush, and has wide interests and even responsibilities; while the second baby has become a rangy, athletic eight-year-old with a wicked sense of humour. 'Back in the days when I was a kid …' I started to say one day, only to be interrupted by Georgia, '… when dinosaurs walked the earth …'

Grandchildren grow away from us just as much as they grow away from their parents and this is how it should be: as the Syrian Maronite poet Kahlil Gibran said, they are not our children, they do not belong to us, but to life expressing itself. And I'm not the only one aware of the tug.

'Oh sorry, Yia-Yia, but I just have to go,' said Cassie, a year or so ago, when I was visiting, and she was being drawn away to her friend's place.

She kept running back and kissing my arm then heading off, turning back before she got to the door, coming back to me, apologising and kissing me again, before finally vanishing outside, into the world that I don't share with her. The world that she shares with her best friend.

IT WAS NOT UNTIL I realised the potential depth and power of the grandmother/grand baby connection, that I finally understood the painful loss Danma must have experienced. Even though I hadn't contacted her for many years, I sat down and wrote to her, expressing my gratitude for her loving kindness to my daughter—and to me—and sorrow at the pain I had caused her by running away, taking my daughter out of her life. I heard later that she was deeply touched by that letter, and carried it around with her for some time. It was the least I could do to make amends. Madeleine was thrilled to be able to show Danma *her* baby, when Cassie arrived, and we visited her several times before she died.

I hope that the grandparents' charter will include clauses to cover this sort of eventuality. It's understandable, especially when there's been a rancorous divorce, that the 'other party's' family might be viewed through a hostile lens. But the connections that children make with grandparents are immensely important and those relationships deserve to be honoured quite separately from anything that parents might create. A recent survey has demonstrated that children with active grandparents in their lives perform better in every area—socially as well as academically. Furthermore, anthropological research suggests that grandparents are probably 'hardwired' to take over parenting in the case of the loss of the mother. Three million years ago, the middle generation of hominins were far more at risk than the older members of the group, who were back in the caves with the young. When the parents didn't come home, quite naturally the grandparent generation would take over.

Millions of years later, the marvellous da Vinci drawing 'St Anne and the Virgin' depicts the later development of this hardwired support: three generations—grandmother, mother and infant—are drawn and it's very clear that Mary, despite being a fully grown woman nursing her own baby, is still sitting on her mother's lap! Instinctively, the great artist knew that a woman needs her own mother's support, not only to help with the next generation, but also as a mother to a daughter as she goes through the powerful—and often overwhelming—experiences that early motherhood brings.

I had no idea what an amazingly powerful experience being a grandmother would turn out to be in my life. Just as childbirth changes a woman's body forever—her voice deepens, her skin pigments differently and sexual responses too are often enhanced—so too, sharing in the birthing and raising of grandchildren, especially when it is one's daughter who gives birth, also seems to have a very powerful psychological effect. The research into the changes at a DNA level that certain states can generate has only just begun. It might well turn out that subtle chemical changes occur in our own bodies and minds as we move into the grandmothering stage, changes that are helpful to our own journey.

Surely, I think, the benefits of the grandmothering relationship must go both ways—enhancing the lives of grandchildren as well as those of grandmothers who share in the development of their grandchildren as they grow. With a young grandchild, we can continue the exciting exploration of life that began with our own birth and developed with our children's births, by learning about things all over again, gaining fresh perspectives, getting down on the floor, in the sand, on the grass, looking at the world in close up as we once did ourselves and then did all over again with our own kids. By taking the time and attempting to answer the huge questions that small children ask, questions that don't always arise in the busy lives we seem to lead these days. And if we can't quite completely '… arrive where we started/And know the place for the first time,'* at least we will have discovered a great deal more.

* T.S. Eliot. 'Little Gidding' (the last of *Four Quartets*)

Lambs' Tongues and Fox Furs

ANGELA CATTERNS

'I'LL RACE YOU TO THE SWING, Angie!' she'd say and we'd run from her back door to the old swing at the end of the backyard.

There were chooks up the back and an old dog called Butch. And even though it felt like it stretched for acres and acres it was really only a suburban backyard in Sydney's inner west. We called her Mimi, but my grandmother's real name was Rose McKnight. Family legend has it that my older brother never could say Grandma properly so somehow he ended up calling her Mimi. As we all did.

A wee small Scottish woman with a slight accent and a heart of gold, Mimi was married to Grandpa. Who would also race me to the swings—and always let me win. He was a veteran of Gallipoli and the Light Horse Brigade.

A tall, handsome New Zealander with a passion for horses—or, more specifically, horse races. Mimi and Grandpa lived around the corner and up the road from us at Strathfield. Our house at the time was white stucco on the outside, theirs was pink. It was a pretty house, with a cottage garden out the front. Pink diosma bushes and those little pale grey plants with soft furry leaves you'd pull off and rub against your cheek and they'd feel like velvet. We called them lambs' tongues.

We'd have Christmas lunch there every year. Mimi would cook a magnificent plum pudding for dessert and insert threepences and sixpences into the slices just before serving them. Into Dad's piece, she'd slide a five-pound note and the family would laugh and shriek when he'd pretend to not know it was there and almost eat it.

When she came to Australia from Glasgow, Mimi lived at Kings Cross and made small felt hats for a living. She embroidered them and sewed beads on them and eventually became a milliner. She opened two shops, one on Church Street, the main street in Parramatta. In the huge cardboard box of photos under Mum's bed, there's a black and white photo of Mimi and her staff—in black skirts and white blouses—standing outside the shop. On the front window is the sign 'R. McKnight Millinery'. She was a wonderful sewer but her eyes were not good and she was never without her little round glasses. Of course in those days one was never to be seen without a hat—everyone wore them. Mimi made all styles: men's, women's, panama straw, felt hats and cloches. She even had a 'hit hat', a comfortable little felt hat which was her best-seller.

The thing I loved most about my grandmother was that she was small, like me. My main memories of her are of the inside of her big cedar wardrobe. From the time I was a toddler she'd let me pick things from it for the purpose of dressing up. And the pickings were rich! Elegant little shoes with high heels and pointed toes. They were only a tiny bit big! Dresses with belts and matching coats. Florals and pleats and embroidery and beads. She never wore trousers. At the foot of her bed was a big white camphor-wood box which held mink jackets and fringed shawls and one of those fox fur stoles with the fox's head still on. It was worn draped around the shoulders and fastened by putting the fox's tail in its own mouth. She had some hats in the house but mainly they were there for her to repair. Each one sat on its own wooden stand and sometimes she'd steam them over a boiling kettle to get them back into shape.

Everything seemed fine to me at the pink house of my grandparents but at some point Mimi and Grandpa split up. I was still just a little kid at the time and none of what was behind this was ever explained to me, and as I grew up I never really wanted to know what had happened to my grandparents' marriage in any case. But I think Mimi had had enough of Grandpa's gambling and spending her money.

For a time Mimi came to live with us, sleeping in the good dining room which was transformed into her bedroom. She was cuddly and soft and I loved getting into bed with her and having her read me stories at bedtime.

One year she went on a big cruise back to Scotland. We waved her off on what seemed an enormous luxurious liner called the *Himalaya*. Months later she arrived home with a suitcase full of gifts and souvenirs. A silver bracelet of charms from everywhere she'd visited for Mum, a little velvet-suited sailor doll with 'Himalaya' embroidered on the front of his cap for me. And among the souvenirs were those beautiful menus with exotic flowers or village scenes hand-painted on the front, from the nights she'd had cocktails and dinner at the Captain's table.

Mimi and Grandpa must have sold their lovely pink house and split the proceeds because Mimi ended up living in a small unit overlooking a park in Ashfield and Grandpa ended up in a dingy little flat up a steep flight of stairs right across the road from the railway line. They were still nearby, now just a couple of train stations away. I'd visit them both on different days of the week after school. Partly because both my parents were working and I needed minding, and also to give them the pleasure of my company, and vice versa.

At Mimi's she'd cook me home-made potato chips and Scottish shortbread and I'd try on more of her clothes. She had long silky nighties and fancy bedjackets that I'd wear to bed in her little spare room. In the morning my school hat would have been cleaned and re-shaped, my uniform cleaned and freshly ironed, and I'd go straight to school from her place.

At Grandpa's the atmosphere was thick with the smoke of too many Craven A cigarettes and his two telephones were always ringing. The radio was on and I'd always have to shoosh when the next race came on. He bought me chocolate éclairs and Juicy Fruit chewing gum and I had an important job to do at his place. I addressed his envelopes. It was never clear to me then but of course he was an SP bookie. I'd put accounts into the envelopes and write his return address on the back. H. Oats. I never did know who H. Oats was. My mother explained years later it was Horse's Oats.

When I was about twelve or thirteen, my grandmother went to hospital. I went to visit her there and vomited in the corridor from the smell and my fear. It was the last time I saw her. She died a long slow death of cancer at the age of sixty-five. My mother was her only child and was distraught. I remember only one thing about her funeral—the way the coffin disappeared on a creaking conveyor belt to an imagined inferno and the curtains closed and that was it.

Grandpa became a regular visitor at our place after that, wearing his hat and carrying a brown suitcase. Inside were more chocolate éclairs and Juicy Fruit. He ended up living till his nineties in the home for War Veterans on Sydney's northern beaches.

WHEN I FINALLY HAD a child of my own, I named her Mimi. At the time I was presenting the *Morning Show* on Triple J and took three months' maternity leave. When I went back to work Mimi was still just a baby. I remember expressing breast milk for her in the toilets at work—motherhood was not yet cool at the youth radio station. My hours were pretty manageable and there was an excellent childcare facility in the ABC building. So Mimi would spend a couple of mornings in childcare, and the rest of the week in the care of her grandmother, my mother Nina. Mum didn't want to be called either Nana or Granny so her grandchildren called her by her first name, Nina, and their grandfather by his first name, Basil, or Ba for short.

Mum was happy and willing to provide this invaluable service, and of course having my daughter cared for by her loving grandmother made me feel secure and comfortable that she was in capable hands. Most days I'd call Mum after the show, just to find out how Mimi was going. What she'd eaten and drunk and whether she'd 'gone down' or not.

Mimi loved going to Nina and Ba's in their beautiful house on the Parramatta River and they loved having her. Mum made Mimi have a nap every day, something most babies and toddlers need, but as a new mum I couldn't quite get it to happen. Perhaps I just wasn't confident enough. Or assertive enough.

At Nina's no nap just wasn't an option. She'd put Mimi down in the little portable cot and wave her magic wand and put her to sleep. Actually it wasn't a magic wand but it was definitely a magic touch. A light caressing of the hair, a little scratching of the back and a song sung soft and low.

Go to sleep my darling
Close your dreamy eyes
Angels up above you
Look at my darling from the skies
Great big moon's a'shining
Stars are in your eyes
Time for little sleepy-heads to go to sleep
That's my lovely little lullaby.

In truth I wouldn't have been able to do it all—keep my fabulous job and have a gorgeous little baby—without my mother's help. Mum loved minding Mimi and knowing she was with her grandmother gave me ultimate peace of mind. She was safe, loved, well-fed *and* she was having a nap. It was a service offered freely by my mother to me, and one for which I was eternally grateful.

When Mimi went to primary school Mum stayed closely involved. For a time she volunteered to read with the children and sometimes would pick her up after school. She and Ba were there at all the assemblies and concerts and special school events too.

Sometimes Mimi would go back to their place after school. She'd sit at her grandmother's dressing table and try on all her jewellery and make-up. She'd open up the big white camphor-wood box at the foot of the bed and play dressings-up with the shawls and scarves, a mink jacket and the old fox stole.

These days, Mimi is a magnificent young woman whose school career is almost over. As a child she loved embroidering and hand-sewing small clothes for her dolls and teddies. In her bedroom she has her own big camphor-wood box full of dressing-up clothes, though these days she wouldn't be seen dead in an old fox fur. And I've always been impressed by how good she looks in hats.

The Other Grandmother

ROBIN BARKER

THE FAT GRANDMOTHER belonged to my mother. She was there when I was born in a country hospital towards the end of the war. My father was still fighting in New Guinea and it would be another eighteen months before he saw me. The day my mother's contractions started the hospital laundress was off sick so the fat grandmother took over the laundry and sang 'Vilia' and 'I Will Take You Home Again Kathleen' in her strong, bosomy voice, feeding the sheets through the wringer as my mother laboured on.

To 'ease the passage' of the crowning of my head my mother's face was covered by an ether mask. When she came to she opened her eyes to a beaming fat grandmother holding me snuggled in to her bountiful breasts. A few years later those titty-boom-booms were a source of giggling wonderment when my sister and I came across the fat grandmother vacuuming her house in the nude.

THE THIN GRANDMOTHER belonged to my father. Early photos show a saucy young woman, one hand on her hip, the other swinging a bag. Her chin is stubborn, her mouth determined, her eyes small and defiant. She had, in todays lingo, attitude.

I inherited my thin grandmother's small eyes and something of the attitude.

MY MOTHER AND I lived with my fat grandmother and my grandfather, until my father came home from the war and we moved to Sydney. As he was a teacher we could escape from the city every school holidays, travelling by night on the creaking, slow-moving North Coast mail to go back to the fat grandmother's house at the beach. I'm not sure how she felt about the way we descended upon her several times a year for prolonged visits but she seemed happy to see us. I loved her and the beach, and the high-stilted old timber house that smelt of soap and polish and salty ocean breezes.

Once, after a week of rain and local flooding, my grandmother donned her voluminous Mac and disappeared into the wet. She bustled in a little later leading an Aboriginal toddler by the hand, his baby sister in her arms. A couple of older siblings and their parents stumbled in after her, shedding water all over the carpets and furniture. My eyes popped with curiosity.

'Please don't stare, Robin. Say hello nicely to Mr and Mrs O'Toole and …' She reeled off the names of the children. 'Their place always floods so they'll be staying here for a while. Let's get everyone into the bath.'

My father looked on with folded arms and no expression.

'Lady of the manor,' he said. 'She'll never get the old fella into the bath.'

A flurry of movement saw us temporarily relocated so they could have the underneath section of the house where we always stayed. To my disappointment, I didn't see much of the family as my sister and I were under strict instructions to keep our distance. They kept to themselves, ate their meals separately and after a few days slipped quietly away.

THE THIN GRANDMOTHER'S early life had been too hard for her to consider the plight of anyone else, let alone the Abos, people she'd been taught to view as a diseased and hopeless lot who got on the grog and wouldn't work.

Her house was miles away from the coast and visits to my thin grandmother were boring—no beach, no swimming, nothing to do—although I enjoyed feeding her chooks and collecting the eggs, intrigued by their warmth and the way the tiny white feathers were glued onto the shells with hen poo.

Visits to the thin grandmother looked up after she swapped the country house for a narrow terrace in an inner Sydney suburb where she took in boarders. Unlike any house I'd ever been in, it had a winding staircase going up three storeys. The small cement backyard had a laundry with leaden-coloured tubs and an outside dunny with an overhead chain just out of my reach. To generate a good enough flush to make everything disappear I had to balance on the rim of the seat, grab the dangling wooden handle in both hands, pull hard then figure out how to climb down without falling in. Neat squares of newspaper hung from a loop of string behind the door. When I needed paper, the thin grandmother gave me some proper stuff off a roll she kept under the stairs.

There were cardboard notices everywhere written in my thin grandmother's laborious sloping hand and hammered into walls with thumbtacks. I'd never been in a house with notices and I liked to read them out loud and ponder over the messages:

'Replace toilet seat after use.'
'Do not leave butts in the yard.'

'No spitting.'

'No baths after 8pm.'

The boarders were single men—New Australians with broken English and glistening hair. On Saturdays they sat around the dining table smoking and listening to the races, speaking in a secret language. My sister and I weren't allowed near them. We were installed in a bedroom upstairs where we passed the time reading and colouring in on a squashy double bed under a mosquito net. Once, during an exploratory venture under the bed we made the thrilling discovery of an enamel pot big enough for a grown-up bottom.

Sometimes I snuck down into the yard, climbed up onto the garbage bin and peeked through the hole in the leaning corrugated-iron gates that opened out into the dunny lane where a gang of kids played. They were different to the kids I was used to; the girls had pierced ears and foxy faces, the boys holey shirts and black knees. Their feet were bare, even in the winter. The girls played hopscotch on big squares drawn on the bitumen in coloured chalk. The boys hooned around on billycarts concocted out of rusting pram wheels and splintery boxes. One summer evening, when the thin grandmother was preparing tea for her boarders, a skinny girl scrambled up the gate from the outside and perched astride the top.

'Whatcher staring at?' A tiny gold cross swung from each ear lobe.

Mortified at being discovered I shrugged. 'The game, the hopscotch.'

'What's ya name?'

I told her.

'Wanna play?'

'Yes … but I can't get out.'

She leaned down. 'Easy, just undo this.' She wrestled with the big bolt at the top of the gate and jiggled it free. 'Now you do the other one. When I get down give the gate a bloody good shove.'

She slithered down and banged on the gate. Excited, I pushed the bolt up and down until it slid out of the keeper. Then I pushed hard until I made a space big enough to wriggle through. My new friend yelled to her mates.

'This's Robin, she's gunna play. Givera taw, Brenda.'

I was no match for them. Their taws hit the right spot every time; mine fell short or overshot. Nimble-footed, they skimmed over the bitumen like barefoot ballerinas. I clunked along in heavy black lace-ups, stepping on lines and tripping over. It didn't matter. I'd never played in the street before and was heady with the thrill of breaking one of my father's strictest rules. Just as I was taking off my shoes and socks the thin grandmother's head poked through the gap in the gate.

'Come here, love.'

Everyone stared.

Embarrassed, I left the game, one shoe on, the other shoe off.

'Time for tea,' my grandmother said. 'Say 'ooray and come in.'

I turned for one last look at the hopscotch, and my taw sitting in number eight.

'Bye,' I said glumly.

''ooray,' the girls shrieked.

Inside, the thin grandmother explained how I wasn't to play in the street and how the dunny lane kids were rough.

'Some of them fathers drink,' she said. 'And when the mothers go out to work them kiddies wag school.'

MY FAT GRANDMOTHER wasn't always fat. Old photos reveal a gracious young woman, tall and slim with a regal posture and a round, sweet face.

She spoke to children seriously as if they were fellow adults. She told us stories and read to us. She played the piano and sang, my sister and I one each side of her nestled in like chicks, although some days a knobbly rigid barrier, the enormous pink corset that we had spied hanging over a chair in her bedroom, came between us and her cuddly flesh. Our favourite song, 'The Little Boy That Santa Claus Forgot' was a desperately sad song about a little boy whose heart is broken because Santa doesn't call at his house. The little boy's request is modest—just some soldiers and a drum. But it is not to be. Christmas Day is a tragic affair where he wanders the streets looking at all the other children playing with their toys before returning home to last year's broken toys. When the second last line of the song reveals that the little boy has no daddy, my sister and I dissolved into heaps of trembling lips and overflowing eyes every time, but we always begged our grandmother to please, please play it again.

THE THIN GRANDMOTHER'S angular figure hardly changed with the passage of time. She just got bonier and bonier.

She didn't sing and never read us stories. She didn't talk much either and when she did she used words that were sometimes incorrect. My parents, particularly my schoolteacher father, were fussy about the way I spoke, to the extent of paying for elocution lessons where I was taught to sharpen up my rounded Australian vowels and recite poems with expression. I was piously aware when my grandmother dropped her aitches and said 'would of' instead of 'would have' and 'done' instead of 'did'.

The thin grandmother also once owned a corset, which she used to bind herself up in to hide an unwanted pregnancy when she was nineteen. This was long before I knew her and a good six years before she gave birth to my father.

THE FAT GRANDMOTHER'S forebears came from England and by the time she was born both sides of her family were well-established middle-class Australians. Her father was a handsome and popular Anglican minister. He preached a decent sermon and rode a pushbike around the parish distributing largesse to the poor and needy. His wife had to keep their personal belongings and food under lock and key as the minister's open-ended generosity was often at the expense of family supplies. My fat grandmother's parents had seven boisterous children and thought they were all special and clever. The minister believed in educating the girls as well as the boys and encouraged them all in sport. He taught his children to swim and to sail in the timber boat he'd built. It was a home where music was important, politics and books were discussed, poetry was recited and where the children were taught to express themselves in an articulate way. My fat grandmother was in the first intake of women to train as teachers in Forest Lodge in Sydney. From her I inherited the joy of a vivid imagination, a passion for reading that to this day is for me life-sustaining, and her hands—sturdy, square-fingered, capable hands. My daughter has them too.

THE THIN GRANDMOTHER'S parents were born into a close-knit Cornish tin-mining community. They migrated to Australia from Cornwall in the late 1880s to a sheep station in western New South Wales where the husband was employed as a boundary rider. The tin-mining life they left behind was hard with an uncertain livelihood and appalling living conditions in tiny, overcrowded, damp cottages. Lung disease, mining accidents and rheumatic fever took the mining folk off, particularly the men, before they were forty.

After they set themselves up in Australia a baby arrived every two years until there were eight kids crammed into the earthen-floored cottage my grandmother's father had built by the creek. The babies stopped coming after his death when, in an inebriated state, he was thrown off his horse on the way home from the pub.

Tin-mining children had a meagre education—the thin grandmother's mother could not write at all and could only just read. But while her children's education was bare-bones in a one-room bush school she made sure they attended every day and got what she'd missed out on.

They were a family of great silences and little talk. The children were whipped around the legs and shoulders for all misdemeanours, major or minor. As they grew up it was common for family members to go for days without speaking, sulking over real or imagined slights. In later life the thin grandmother and one of her sisters didn't speak a single word to each other for twenty years, maintaining their sisterly muteness until death.

The children's education was over by the end of primary school—the boys went off to work as station-hands, the girls as station cooks or domestics. The sheep station where my grandmother found employment was a huge concern with its own school, slaughtering yards, shearing sheds, stables, staff quarters and vegetable garden. Photos from the time she was there show her employer, a portly grazier, suited up like a Victorian gentleman alongside his wife, decked out in a flowing gown and wide-brimmed hat, standing in their garden among the roses with several overdressed children at their feet.

THE FAT GRANDMOTHER never taught school again after she married an austere, abstemious third generation Australian of Scottish ancestry, a World War I veteran. A bushman who worked for the Forestry, he spent a lot of time away from home, had a way with animals, spoke sparingly and closely supervised every penny my fat grandmother spent. On a brighter note, he always made sure there was plenty of chopped dry wood for the stove, and the fat grandmother was first in the district to get an electric washing machine.

They had four healthy children. The fat grandmother clucked over them, taught them good manners, helped them with their schoolwork, cooked, scrubbed, cleaned and nursed them through their illnesses. The children were big talkers, highly imaginative and bright. They had, in many ways, an idyllic childhood near the coast by a river where they breathed pristine air, swam in clear unpolluted water, roamed the countryside, rode horses, and had chooks and dogs for friends. But inside, the home was often threaded with anxiety. Chaos descended when it all got too much for my grandmother, weighed down by the strain of her workload, her bad health and the hovering tensions that accumulate when two mismatched people have to share their lives.

WHEN THE THIN GRANDMOTHER became pregnant she told no one and no one knew. Strong and reliable, her work didn't suffer and the corset kept her figure slim. She gave birth one night, on her own, in her small bedroom off the kitchen. When the squatter and his family bounced down for breakfast on that mild, spring morning it was to a silent, empty kitchen and no cook.

What happened when my grandmother and her baby were found? Was she treated kindly? Did someone clean her up and make her a cup of tea? Were curious children shushed and sent outside to play? Was there any sniggering behind the astonishment and concern of the faces circling her bed as she lay there with the baby? My grandmother was a woman of few words so I'd be sure she didn't have much to say—or give a clue as to who the father might be.

In any event, as soon as was considered proper my grandmother and her baby were dispatched, by horse and sulky, back to her mother. The baby, born with a mild paralysis of one side, paid a price for her concealment. My grandmother's response to her birth was a silent, rebellious anger. She handed the baby over to her mother and slammed the book shut on that chapter of her life.

Six years later in another town a long way away from her mother, her child and the sheep station, the thin grandmother, a Protestant, married my grandfather in an unadorned room in the presbytery of the local Catholic Church. The man she married was a charming, freckled drover who had a magic touch with horses. Of Irish-Australian extraction he came from up north, way out west—marginal country—from a family where the boys disappeared without a backward glance, rarely seen or heard from again. He and my grandmother lived in a small weatherboard cottage in a tiny settlement on the edge of station country. My father arrived not long after the marriage and three years later another boy was born. The thin grandmother loved her plump gurgling boys. She slept with them and breastfed each one for years.

One day the thin grandmother's elder sister turned up with a nine-year-old girl.

'Here's your kid,' she said. 'Now Ma's passed on you must take her. She's your responsibility.'

The child was small and scrappy, shrunken on one side. She was confused because the person she knew as her Ma was gone and she wasn't sure who this grim lady with the wild black hair was supposed to be.

In the thin grandmother's mind the pregnancy, the corset, the pain, the shame, the birth, the aftermath, was a nightmare she'd removed herself from long ago—it had never happened.

'No,' she said. 'She's nothing to do with me.'

But the sister stood her ground and left without the child.

I suspect it was unpleasant when the charming, freckled husband came home and heard the thin grandmother's terse explanation. It's hard to imagine that he showed too much understanding about the sudden arrival of his wife's illegitimate child. Apart from another mouth to feed and the bitter taste of supporting another man's child, there was the local gossip the girl's appearance would generate.

Maybe I do him an injustice. Maybe he was fine about it. But after he died from pneumonia six months later, my grandmother destroyed all his photos and never spoke of him again. My father and his brother grew up knowing nothing about their father—what he looked like, where he came from, his cleverness with horses or even that my grandmother loved him very much. Stories about the charm, the love and the horses filtered down, ghostlike, from contact with distant relatives long after the boys were adults, not from my grandmother. The only tangible evidence we have that he existed at all are the freckles he passed down to my father and me, which no one else on either side of my family has.

The thin grandmother was now on her own with three children and no income. I don't know what she lived on for the next couple of years until the widow's pension and child endowment arrived in 1926 but she didn't put the children into an orphanage, as was common then for women in her plight.

Once both boys were in school she cooked in hotels and boarding houses, leaving her sons to their own devices for several nights a week. Rabbits were the staple food, which the boys supplied. From the ages of six and nine they went out early every evening to set the traps, then out again twice more, around three and six in the morning, to release the traps and bring home the dead bunnies for food and skins.

I knew something about my father's childhood from snippets I gleaned over the years—mostly from my mother. But not long before he died, he uncharacteristically revealed a lot more for a tape recording, never complaining, simply stating the facts, chuckling at times over childhood incidents I was secretly saddened, even appalled by.

The house my father grew up in had no books, no toys, no music and not much conversation. Food was in short supply. At times they ate nettles, alfalfa and wild mushrooms. Clothes were scanty, feet were bare, the routine medical treatment for everything from whooping cough to broken limbs was a dose of Epsom salts. Nevertheless, the boys grew up loving their mother and in their adult lives always looked out for her, and never spoke ill of her.

All my life, even as an adult, my father never uttered a word to me about the girl, his sister. But she was there all along, a presence in their home for several of his childhood years, a constant reminder of my grandmother's disgrace and fear.

She was kept away from her half brothers. She wasn't allowed to play or eat with them. She went to school briefly when she first arrived but it couldn't have been much fun as, having had little education, she was put into a class with children several years younger than she was. She was grubby, uncared for and malnourished. Her teeth, decayed and rotting, were all removed and not replaced with dentures.

Eventually the thin grandmother gave up on the girl's schooling and took her to work with her to help with the cooking. When the girl reached adolescence her mother passed her on to a local family where she did home duties in return for her board. At eighteen she fled the town for the city.

THE FAT GRANDMOTHER died exhausted at sixty-three when I was ten. I was taken to see her in the hospital a few days before she died. She sat propped up on a teetering pile of pillows, each breath an effort. I gave her the rainbow-coloured autograph book I'd been given for Christmas and she managed to write in it: 'Be good sweet maid.' And gave me a wink.

The afternoon she died, I saw my grandfather lean on her piano and sob into his arms. My mother was trying to comfort him. I wasn't aware that men cried, let alone my towering, invincible grandfather, and went outside. I sat on the steps and put my hands over my ears.

Soon my red-eyed mother took me to a neighbour's house for an overnight visit. The parents took us fishing. We caught hundreds of whiting without even baiting the hooks. We just hurled the lines in, laughing wildly at the madness of racing up the beach and falling harmlessly into the sand with yet another dopey fish jerking and flapping along behind. The reckless laughter eased the scary band around my chest.

Everyone agreed funerals were no place for children so I didn't go. Apparently the church was packed. I loved my fat grandmother. Everyone did. My children would have too, but of course they never met her.

PHYSICALLY AND EMOTIONALLY as tough as old boots, the thin grandmother outlived two of her children, all but one of her siblings and most of her friends so her funeral, when she died at ninety-nine, was a quiet affair with a handful of people.

When I was a child, my fat grandmother's softness and tender magic didn't leave much space inside my head for my thin grandmother's bony reticence and raspy edges. But in the last twenty years of her life, when I lived near her, we spent a lot of time together and I discovered she was good company. She never complained—even when her fading eyesight made life difficult—and was always delighted to see me, with never a word of reproach when it had been a while between visits.

More demonstrative and openly affectionate with her great-grandchildren than she'd been with her sons and grandchildren, they knew her well. She played with them and yarned to them, and gently chastised me when she thought I was being too tough on them.

A few years ago her daughter's family got in touch with my sister. By then the thin grandmother was long dead and at that stage my sister and I had never heard the story of her only daughter, my father's half sister.

When she fled the country town where she'd lived for five years after leaving my grandmother's house she was—so the story goes—pregnant to the local bootmaker. She left in the company of a grandmotherly woman who had taken her under her wing. The woman bought her clothes and dentures, and helped her through the pregnancy and birth. The staff at the hospital where she gave birth tried to make her give the baby up but she refused to part with him. Eventually she married; her husband adopted her son and twelve years later they had a baby girl. Outwardly, her life was stable and fulfilling. Inwardly, the bleak memories of her fractured childhood often made her feel 'down'. She also had the paralysis to deal with—never knowing what caused it, believing it may have been polio.

Her daughter, the cousin I never knew I had until recently, grew up with the spectre of my grandmother, always referred to as the 'witch', haunting her family even before she was born. When my cousin was about ten she was alarmed (and strangely thrilled) by her mother's sudden decision to take the family on a journey back to the witch's abode somewhere out in the country. The thought of actually meeting this fearful, but creepily fascinating, ghost made her sick with excitement and dread, fearing the witch might cast an evil spell on them all. When they finally found her abode, a sad little cottage at the edge of a vast yellow-stubbled paddock, and discovered she was no longer there, my cousin wasn't sure if she was relieved or disappointed.

'That mad trip,' my cousin said to me when we finally met, 'was all about Mum wanting to let her mother know she was doing okay and ...' she paused, 'to show her that she'd managed to get a good life despite her. And I think she probably wanted to show us off as well.'

The thin grandmother and her daughter never did make contact. At one stage they lived only a couple of Sydney suburbs apart so they could have found one another, I suppose. But one didn't care to and the other was too frightened to.

THE DISCOVERY of the thin grandmother's daughter years after they had both died came as a great surprise to me. My mother and father must have known about her all along but refused to discuss it. Unwed pregnancies were disastrous for women of my era too so I have great sympathy for the nightmare my grandmother faced. But a chill settles between my shoulder blades every time I think of her treatment of her daughter.

I have to remind myself that I have no idea how I would behave raising children in such precarious circumstances, struggling day to day with barely any money, no family support, no medical care. I've never lived like this for a day, let alone ten years. I like to think I'd do the right thing, especially in relation to my children, but in all honesty I don't know. I've inherited enough of the thin grandmother's stubbornness and toughness, traits that can be good or bad, to be uncertain of what I might do in a similar situation.

My grandmother's daughter never knew exactly why her mother hated her so much. I don't either. It remains a sad, incomprehensible puzzle for me, obscured by the haziness of family memory genuine and deliberate. The truth of their story, lost in that twilight between the real and the imagined, can never really be known.

Ronny Boy

RUBY LANGFORD GINIBI

NGANYAH GRAND JAHJAM, my grandchild Ronny Boy, was born on the seventh day of the seventh month 1977, which is supposed to be lucky, or so people say. But it wasn't all that lucky a birth date for my third eldest grandson, Ronald James Nicholas.

My daughter Ellen is Ronny's mother and in the 1970s both she and Ronny's father—a whitefella—worked at the Prince Alfred Hospital in Camperdown in Sydney. Ellen was a 'pink lady', bringin the food around to patients. Ron, her partner, was a wardsman, who was later sacked for smokin on the job.

When baby Ronny was about two weeks old Ellen and Ron asked me to look after him while they worked. Ronny Boy was a lovely little thing, seven or eight pounds in weight when he was born, with blond fuzzy hair and hazel eyes. I was so proud of him. They'd take him off me on the weekends. Which was okay with me, cause one of my other daughters, Pauline, had a baby too by then. She'd given birth on 20 June that same year to her eldest child, my grand-daughter Roberta Pearl, who was just under three weeks older than Ronny Boy.

So my house was alive again with babies crying and gurgling and doing baby poos, and with titty bottles and teats sterilising in a big boiler on the stove. And the copper was always bubbling with terry towelling nappies and all kinds of baby stuff, while my youngest son Jeffery, who was about eight years old at this time, was off at school. These were happy family days and I ended up looking after little Ronny for one and a half years, until Ellen and her Ron moved away to Blackett, a suburb in Mount Druitt, in far western Sydney to start their own lives. And when Pauline and Roberta did likewise and moved a bit later themselves to Lethbridge Park, I had the place to myself again.

Some years later, in 1987, after I'd moved to Allawah Hostel at Granville after major surgery, I used to visit Ellen and her partner where they were still living at Blackett. By then they'd had four childen together, but Ronny was the only boy. Sometimes I'd go to visit them. I'd see Ron Senior of a weekend when he wasn't working. He'd be bouncing the girls Tara and Lee and Toni on his knee. And big brother Ronny, who was about nine or ten by now, would be looking on lovingly with his hopeful eyes watchin and thinkin, 'When ya gonna bounce me, Dad?' He'd be in great expectation of his dada bouncing him on his knee too. But it didn't happen. Ever.

It broke my heart to see it, so one day I said, 'Give ya son a go, Dad.'

'Don't you come here telling me what ta do and psychoanalysing me,' Ron Senior retorted.

What a pig, I thought.

But later my Ellen told me that when he was a kid himself, Ron Senior, the eldest child in his family, had to be responsible for his younger brothers and sisters. He had to look after them and make sure they never fell over and hurt themselves. In those days kids were sent outside to play so they couldn't listen in when there were visitors and the grown-ups were talking. And if Ron wasn't responsible for the little ones, Ellie explained, he was chucked against the wall by his drunken father. Ron Senior's own father eventually told me more or less the same story. If Ron didn't look after his siblings properly he'd get belted.

Well, there ya go! I thought.

The pattern had repeated itself with Ron's own son, and now he couldn't show Ronny Boy, who let's face it was still only a kid, any love or affection. It says in the Bible that the sins of the fathers fall back on the children, and here it was, happening with some of my own mob. It tore me apart.

Not surprisingly, Ronny Boy couldn't handle his father's very stern attitude to life either, or the way he treated him. And his mother, my Ellen, was continually rowing with his father too, on account of his treatment of little Ronny. When he was about ten or eleven years of age Ronny Boy rebelled against all this, causing all sorts of strife. And by the time he was in his early teens he was falling into various sorts of bigger trouble and was in and out of boys' homes. He was in Bidwell for a while, and was sexually abused in there. At one point he was diagnosed as having Attention Deficit Disorder, and then he took to drugs.

After about sixteen years together, Ellen and Ron the father broke up. While Ronny Boy had been in one of the boys' homes, his father took Ellen and the girls and they moved to Coonabarabran, a town out west in NSW. But Ron Senior couldn't find any work out there and so he left Ellen stranded on her own in Coona with the girls. She rang me and asked me for petrol money so she could come back to Sydney, and luckily I had some spare funds then so I sent her some cash. She and the girls moved into a women's refuge in Sydney, the Miriam Centre at Enmore. Ellie had got sick and tired by then of all the battlin and fightin with Ronny's father. She was always pleadin with him to treat young Ronny better, like a son. She and the girls ended up staying at the refuge until her application was processed and she got a Housing Commission home at Miller, in Green Valley.

By then Ronny Boy was outa the homes and went to livin back with his mum and his three sisters. He'd have been about sixteen or seventeen by now, and everything was okay for a while. But soon the stress of raisin a family all on her own started to depress Ellie and she started to drink a lot, which she never did before. Talk about ya past catchin up with ya! She reminded me of what I was like when I lost three of my kids through tragic circumstances. I hit the piss terrible, I must tell ya, and nearly drank myself stupid until my four daughters bailed me up and brought me to my senses.

Anyway, during this time Ellie met an Irishman named Connor in a pub somewhere. He was an engineer, and a heavy drinker too, as most Irish seem to be. He was a good provider though, and wanted to adopt Ellie's girls as his own. One night though, when Ellie and Connor got back from the pub, Ronny Boy had a big row with Connor about him encouragin his mum to drink so much. Ronny flattened Connor with a baseball bat and next thing he was charged with assault. So it was back to the boys' homes for him. He ended up in Cobbin Boys' Home at Penrith.

By the time Ronny was discharged after the assault on Connor, I'd moved from Allawah Hostel and was living in Eagle Vale, near Campbelltown, west of Sydney. Young Jeffery was my full-time carer then, and he went and picked Ronny up from the boys' home and brought him back to my place because he had nowhere else to go. Jeff helped him get a job, and it was good for young Ronny to be among family. And I was happy to have him back under my roof once again.

Ronny saved some money and purchased a bike, and Jeff was helping him fix it up for registration. Then, lo and behold, he goes and steals a car one time when he was off his face. He crashes it into a utility, accidentally killing a young man. So when the cops catch up with him it's back into an institution yet again—this time though it was prison, on a charge of manslaughter.

By the time he was sentenced, Ronny's mother and her bloke had moved to Parramatta. Ellen never fronted up in court to support her son because it stressed her so much. And besides, she was still drinking like there was no tomorrow.

Unfortunately, I wasn't able to go either. I was so stressed out by the whole business I ended up in hospital. I'd had a bad asthma attack and was in there for over a week. By the time I was discharged, my grandson had been taken off to jail.

I'M DISTRESSED almost every single day of my life about my grandson. For six years Ronny Boy was incarcerated in Junee prison down near the Victorian border. He'd served nearly all of his sentence for manslaughter, before he was brought back to serve out the rest in Long Bay prison near Malabar in eastern Sydney.

I'd already gone through the grief of having one of my own sons in jail for nearly twenty years for something he never did. At seventeen and a half years of age, my Nobby was the eldest in a group of teenagers that was pulled over by the cops. The police were after a conviction for a crime that had been committed in the area, and Nobby was the one who copped it. The charge against him was attempted murder and escaping lawful apprehension, even though nobody was actually murdered or maimed.

Ronny Boy had already served most of his sentence for the manslaughter charge and was about to be paroled. It was only then that the police came up with some new DNA evidence against him, which led to another seven years being added on to his time behind bars. Ronny's in his early thirties now as I write this, so where is his hope of living any sort of good life outside prison walls?

I never really expected my Ellen would go to the jail much to visit her only son Ron, let alone that his father would, although I believe he did just the once. Over the years Ellie and the girls, Ronny's sisters, have been to visit him a few times. But I couldn't let my grandson down like his parents had. I have seen what prison has done—and continues to do—to my people.

For years while he was servin his sentence I was the only contact with family my grandson Ronny Boy had. And these days I am still the only real connection to our mob that he has. I send him money for his buy-ups. I bought him a television, even some clothing—track shoes, and some tracksuit pants, always in jungle green, as well as socks and undies. His uncles Jeff and Nobby have helped me from time to time with the finances for this. But sadly, Ronny Boy's mother is drinking heavily still, on account of her ongoing stress.

Me and my wheelchair went to see Ronny Boy once not so long back, when he was at Long Bay, with Jeffery pushin me the whole way from the car park to the visitin centre. It was a big effort all round, but I know Ronny Boy really appreciated seeing his uncle and grandmother.

Ronny Boy has an eleven-year-old son, Tristan, who's autistic. Ronny tells me that he and the boy's mother have decided they are going to try to make a life together when he gets out of the jail in about a year and a half's time.

And now I hear my grandson Ronny has found God and become a born-again Christian. He had always been a believer when it came to spiritual things. He believes there's a good spirit who looks after everything, and that we live in unity and harmony with Mother Earth, and that we always have because she's nurtured us forever. And Ronny Boy's drug-free now too, he tells me.

It's heartbreaking for Ronny being incarcerated though, not seeing his son, or any other family. And it's heartbreaking for me too, who he calls 'Gumi', which is Bundjalung for grandmother. When he rings me from prison I tell him, 'Be strong, Ronny Boy. You gotta be strong.' And I tell him, 'May the good spirit of our Aboriginal Dreamin watch over you forever.'

But still, every time I think of my incarcerated grandson, I ask myself: where is justice for us Kooris in our own land? We do not live in a real democracy or have any proper human rights so long as we are still the most jailed people in this country. My people make up not quite two per cent of the total population of Australia but we have been imprisoned so much. You just need to look at the statistics. They'll tell ya! We Aboriginal people cannot be the baddest, most evil people in Australia, aye?

I've been writing about the incarceration of Indigenous Australians and Aboriginal deaths in custody since this country's population was seventeen million, and now it's around twenty million. And I'll keep on writing. I'll keep on caring for my grandson too. Ronny Boy is the only grandchild that is very close to me, and I hope to live long enough to see him released from jail and settled with his little family. After all he's been through I really hope there's a happy ending for him—and that he can find that elusive thing called love. Meanwhile, I just keep on waiting until the day he gets out of prison and comes back home.

Grandma's Tree

CAITLIN ADAMS

MY MOTHER did not hold Isaac upside down by his ankles behind her back saying, 'Where's Isaac?' She did not push and spin him on the tyre swing, laughing loudly. She did not buy him a plastic tricycle with buttons that made engine sounds and honks when pushed. She did not try to teach him the proper order in which to stack the multi-coloured rings on a pole.

My mother gave Isaac a little yellow mechanical pencil that matched her own. When she was writing notes, editing a draft or making to-do lists, he would sit on the floor and mimic her, sketching intricate webs on tiny sheets of notepaper. She read nursery rhymes to him: 'Wee Willy Winky runs through the town / Upstairs, downstairs, in his nightgown.' She sat nearby and watched him, sometimes joining in or asking questions, as he played with his small stuffed animals, one in each hand; in the tradition of his grandma, he told stories, having his animals climb furniture and fall down, murmuring dialogue. And she took him to the playground.

'I DON'T THINK of him as being mine,' says my mother of my newborn son. 'I think of him as being yours.' She sounds surprised, as if she expected to be possessive. Isaac is three weeks old.

My mother stayed with us for the first month of Isaac's life. She arrived the week before my due date to be sure she was here in time. Roughly once a year she came to visit, travelling to the States from Sydney, where she had returned to live after twenty-five years of living in New York City. She shuttled on Amtrak between Washington, DC, where I live, and New York, where the bulk of her American friends live. In consideration of the distance travelled, she would stay with us for weeks on end.

Her theory was that, in general, most relatives and friends—grandmothers among them—showed up and wanted to hold the new baby, leaving the mother to do the entertaining and washing up. But this may have been based on her own experience as a new mother. She told me the story of renting a summer house with my father when I was two months old. She was in the kitchen washing the dishes from dinner and the baby bottles I had used that day. The window over the sink opened on to the deck, where my father and their guests were drinking wine. She overheard my father talking. 'We share the parenting and housekeeping fifty-fifty,' he said. She cried.

My mother wanted me to hold Isaac. So she did the laundry and dishes. Learning how to use the unfamiliar espresso machine, she even made her own coffee.

'Is it wrong that I want to hold him all the time?' I ask her. I'm sitting cross-legged on the couch with tiny sleeping Isaac nestled in the crook of my arm.

'He is lucky to have you, my darling,' she replies from the kitchen.

As a newborn, Isaac fell asleep only when being held, usually by me. He didn't sleep for long stretches either, and only I could reliably and sustainably console him. Often, he would not transfer to the crib or he would wake after a mere twenty minutes. My mother would take over, sit on a chair on the back deck in good weather (or lie on the couch in not-so-good weather), with her feet up on another chair and Isaac asleep across her chest, his head on her shoulder. She would let him take his whole nap on her—sometimes for longer than an hour. She would read over his little body—one arm around him, the other hand holding her book.

Three weeks postpartum, I had the go-ahead to run again. I needed to run. My mother urged me to go; she knew better than anyone (except maybe my husband, but

I do write 'maybe'). So I headed out. Isaac was asleep in his vibrating seat, with a Fisher-Price plastic fish tank making wave sounds beneath him.

I took the dog and the mobile phone with me. About forty minutes later I got a call from her. 'He's up; he's crying.'

'I'm heading back.' I was twenty minutes away and hoped the new grandmother would cope.

By the time I ran through the door, she had the faux fish tank propped up on the counter, now tuned to a baby-ified version of some Mozart piece, and had Isaac cradled in her arms. He was not quite crying; his eyes were open, and he was making a low-level fuss. But he was not howling. She was singing the lyrics in German. I was not surprised that she recognised the piece and knew the words—she always seemed to. My mother knew many languages: Indonesian, French and Italian, in addition to German. And she was an opera fan, from her childhood in Sydney throughout her adulthood. She kept the playbills as proof and reference—stacks and stacks of them stored in boxes.

Months later, when Isaac saw his grandmother next, she sang that song (I wish I could remember it), and he lifted his tiny foot as if frozen in the middle of a ballet move, holding on to the couch cushion as his bar.

'Oh, look!' she exclaimed. 'He remembers.'

She would sing it whenever she saw him after a long absence, to check if he remembered. He reliably lifted his foot.

I remember my mother usually had music playing in our flat in New York City—the radio tuned to the classical public radio station. She recognised most pieces. 'Oh, that's so and so's such and such,' she'd say. She also knew the words—in the original language. And she would sing them.

She also sang show tunes in a clear, jaunty voice that carried well in the flat, often while she was in the kitchen, and pre-rock pop tunes such as 'You're the top' and 'Button up your overcoat'. I remember getting older—becoming a teenager—and yelling at her to stop, embarrassed even though no one else was there.

'ISN'T HE LOVELY?' she repeatedly asks, or states, while observing Isaac at different stages.

She had this annoying, polite, conversational habit of phrasing statements as questions. If I step back and think about this habit, I realise that she was encouraging participation, mine in this case. She loved observing and discussing the small things of life (say, the reaction to a bad haircut or what a good haircut would look like), as well as bigger questions of politics and philosophy.

I ask, 'Does he remind you of me?'

'I suppose. It is hard to remember.'

But she remembers everything. I want her to say, 'Oh, yes, he is exactly like you.' Not because she says he is lovely—she tells me I am lovely, too—but because I want that continuity and connection. Isaac may be male, but I want him, my first child, to look and be just like me, for better or worse.

My great-grandmother, grandmother, my mother and I share the same middle name, Emily, which I could not pass on to Isaac. Giving him the male Emile seemed to stretch the tradition, and besides I thought I might have a daughter one day. So my son's middle name is his grandmother's maiden name—Felton. As Isaac's features matured, my mother would greet him with 'Hullo, Felton-baby'. He was broad of face, and had a big smile and eyes that crinkled, just like hers and her brother's.

ISAAC WAS A TINY BABY and still small as a toddler. At one-and-a-half, he went through a battery of tests for possible 'failure to thrive'. The specialist threatened me with a feeding tube in his stomach if he did not drink two prescribed calorie-packed drinks a day. I knew I had no hope of getting food into my son without entertainment. So I set him up with a baby DVD on a mini player for mealtimes.

When I was a toddler, my mother bought a kiddie-sized set of a wicker table and chairs so I would sit still and eat. She put them in the corner of our living room, bordered on two sides by the French doors and fire escape. Her plan didn't work. Between meals, I did pretend 'restaurant' at the table, using modelling clay, rolling, layering, slicing and serving multicoloured 'meals'. She also tried plates and bowls with pictures, such as those of Winnie the Pooh. She hoped I would eat all my food eagerly to get to the bottom. This plan also didn't work. Maybe Isaac's eating issues were cosmic revenge for my own.

Soon after the tests (which later all came back as normal), Isaac and I flew to Sydney to visit Grandma—his first time abroad. My mother borrowed a sleek white highchair, in which I would try to feed Isaac. At mealtimes, he'd clamp his mouth shut, as I had come to expect. I had tricks, but one day I was done trying. I wanted to throw his food across the room.

'You go out,' his grandmother said. 'I'll feed him.'

I did as she suggested; I was no longer useful.

On my return to her flat, she confessed. 'I was cruel. I feel terrible. I closed the screen on his little DVD player if he would not take a bite. I was very stern. Only if he took a bite could he watch again. I must have opened and closed it twenty times. It worked. But I feel terrible.'

I looked at Isaac. He did not appear traumatised as he climbed the back of a large red chair and laughed, proud of his accomplishment. But my mother avoided feeding him from then on.

EVEN BEFORE HE COULD WALK, Isaac has always been on the go and, to this day, he does not stop. I do not exaggerate. He was—and is still—like an Energizer Bunny. Once, when Isaac was two and my mother was visiting, he was desperately in need of activity. We'd all pay if he did not get that activity. Stuffed and plastic animals would be no longer played with, but thrown backwards, one by one, over his shoulders. Any remaining tower built of blocks would be knocked down. Fits would be pitched over the slightest thing—Mama was on the phone; Daddy closed the door; Isaac could not find the matching shoe that was right in front of him.

Generally, my mother was not quick to step in, but she did sense if and when it was necessary. When staying with us, she would distract Isaac with a book or a song, inviting him to sit with her on the couch. And he would do it, be mellow with her. When I had a heavy, last-minute editing job or a looming deadline for an article her skills were especially required. As they were if I was losing my patience. And I do mean losing it. Completely. Yelling as a release rather than a solution. Sometimes, and I am not proud of this, I have screamed so loud I'm sure the neighbours could hear. I have screamed because I wanted to leave and be by myself. I have screamed because saying 'go to sleep' or 'leave me alone for a minute' did not work.

More than once, after she'd gone home, I'd call her in Sydney and say, 'I lost it, Mum. He wouldn't take a nap, and he's so tired. He wouldn't eat, and he's hungry. And

I need a moment alone. And I have not gone running. And the house is a mess. I hate this.' I could work myself up to tears as the list went on and on. A downward spiral, my mother would call it.

I expected her to try to calm me down because she was usually so with me, not to chastise me. But she did neither. When I described yelling at my first child she simply said, 'Good for you. You don't need to be perfect, and he needs to know.' This coming from the mum who wrote of me at six months old: 'Doesn't cry much; crying not piercing.' Clearly, she was biased.

AS A YOUNGER WOMAN, my mother often felt she had to be quiet, polite and reserved. As a twenty-something, she was quiet with my father's arm around her shoulders in an Upper West Side bar while he went on and on about being a socialist or spoke flawless French when they lived in Brussels. As a thirty-one-year-old expectant mother, she listened to her male obstetrician who encouraged natural childbirth, stressing its naturalness. But he gave her no concrete tools to deal with the pain, and she did not feel it was okay to scream. Making it easier for the doctor was prominent in her mind, though she also resented this concern, and she felt guilty that he had opera tickets for that night in May. After she had laboured for a full day, exhausted and unable to push (wanting to die, she said), she was put under general anaesthetic, and I was pulled out with forceps. My father still reminds me of my 'banana head'.

And even with me, the only child of a single mother, she was by nature understanding and, some other mothers thought, too permissive. But I do remember one particular occasion when I was four years old and had asked for a tuna fish sandwich for lunch. I was a fussy eater—the only sandwiches I would eat were tuna or peanut butter (no jam—too sticky). This day, once my mother had made the sandwich, I said, 'I don't want *that*,' as if she had prepared something horrible that I would never, ever think of eating. I may have whined; I may have demanded something else. I don't remember. I do remember the brown glazed coffee mug that she smashed on the kitchen floor. My mother burst into tears and picked me up, hugging me, apologising. I don't remember her cleaning up the shards.

Another time (I don't recall what I did), my mother chased me down the thirty-foot hall in our flat. I knew that, if she caught me, she was going to spank me. And she didn't spank, ever. I don't even remember her ever sending me to my room. When she at last caught me, I sat down in the dark hallway, holding on to the tufts of green wall-to-wall carpeting and keeping my bum on the floor with all my might. She did not spank me.

When I retold these stories—and I enjoyed repeating these memories and discussing them with her—she would say, 'Oh, I traumatised you.' And she would sigh. 'I wish I had not gotten so angry.' Yet I am almost fond of these memories, the exceptions to the rule of an understanding mother.

And when I became frustrated, angry, with my child, my mother would take care of both of us by whisking her grandson away to the playground. She'd grab the little red umbrella stroller, strap him in and walk up the steep hill to the halfway point, then they'd turn right and head downhill to the park with the playground. Just a short walk, no more than ten minutes. I can do it in five, but I am usually walking fast, either in a rush or trying to get a bit of exercise value out of it. These days, Isaac insists that I run there as I'm pushing him, regardless of the fact that he now, at four, is getting too heavy for me to propel him up a steep hill and could easily do the walk himself with no stroller.

On an early visit to the playground, maybe even her first, my mother took off with Isaac while I put on some loud music and got to work. On the way out, after cresting the hill, she spotted a hollow, but very much alive, tree. A tree with green leaves spread on broad branches that reached, leaned out, into the narrow street. We live in a so-called 'Tree City USA' (a sign on the main street proclaims the town has earned this title for ten years running) that has many old, large and beautiful trees. Isaac was happy in the stroller, and my mother was enjoying the walk, the sights of our little suburban town. My mother noticed this particular tree because it had a large A-frame hollow at its base. Doing this very same walk countless times, I'd not been aware of the hollow. But my mother, a writer alert to the unique details of inanimate objects, as she was attuned to such qualities in people, spotted it.

My mother was fascinated with this tree; things could be hidden in it. She immediately saw its potential for secrets and stories. She unbuckled Isaac and showed the hollow to him. On the way home, they put in a stick that he had been playing with.

The next time she took him to the playground, they picked some daisies from our front yard to stash in the hollow. My mother played up the tree. 'Oh, here is that special tree where we can hide things, keep them safe just for us.' Once again, she let Isaac out of the stroller. On his knees, he removed the stick—to play with again—and put the daisies in.

ISAAC LOVES SMALL PLASTIC DINOSAURS. He has, oh, hundreds of them because I cannot stop buying them. They are cheap and fun, and I am drawn to making collections. (This is also why we have a basket full of little metal cars.) To this day, Isaac will line up the dinosaurs (or cars) across carpets and tables—and refuse to put them away. After Isaac went to sleep at night, my mother would set up dinosaur tea parties for him to find when he came down the steps first thing in the morning. Those he knocked down.

On their next walk to the playground, my mother, sly and quick, slipped one of Isaac's tiny dinosaurs into the hollow on the way to the playground. On the way home, she asked Isaac, 'Do I see something in that tree?' Loosed, he ran over; kneeling in front of the hollow, he peered in. And there was a little orange pteranodon. The tree was now magic.

MY MOTHER DANCED around belief in the supernatural or even in an afterlife. She didn't go to church and had no particular or codified faith. She described the vivid and frightening hellfire sermons from her days of being sent to Sunday school as being traumatising for her, and told me that her mother quickly made the decision to take her out. Was she Anglican? I hardly know. Certainly she never took me to church. When she was first diagnosed with ovarian cancer, however, my mother wrote a note to me: 'I'll watch over you, and just think of me and how I love you.' Isaac also has not been to church with me, and doesn't go to Sunday school, though attending nursery school in the local Methodist church has left him with the belief that, as he puts it, 'God is in the church.' He also says, 'Grandma's in the sky.' He said this for the first time after she died, but maybe all he means is that we travelled by airplane to get to her.

After her death, I hoped she could live on in some conscious way. But I doubt there's an afterlife, a means for my mother to watch over me as she had promised. 'Come on, Mum,' I think, especially when I have almost picked up the phone to call her, usually in the late afternoon, which would have been her morning in Sydney. A sign? Something in my peripheral vision? A dream? I have had four:

Leaning on pillows, she is sitting up in bed, in what appears to be a bright, cheerful hospital room. She is dressed in one of her woven cotton dressing gowns, white with a dark blue Chinese print. She tells me not to forget what my father had left for me in our New York City flat: the yellow toy dog and Sesame Street bookends, left on the high shelf framing the living room walls. I have no idea what she is talking about—these items do not exist—though I suddenly have a photo-perfect vision of them. I tell her she looks and sounds great. She is bright eyed and full of face, has a strong, clear voice, and has her classic layered bob haircut. She looks at me with a calm smile, as if to say, 'Of course I do, now.'

I am staying in a vacation house in a forest, near water, on stilts. My in-laws are there. My father is there. The house is a mess. Every room has a sink full of dirty dishes. Muck adheres to patches of floor. I can't find what I needed in my suitcase, so I am not fully dressed. My mother calls, or I call her. Either way, I have a phone to my ear and can hear her voice. Her voice is reassuring, but

I cannot decipher what she says. And then she isn't on the line anymore. Either I can't hear her or she is no longer responding.

I am standing near a wall with mirrors of many different sizes and shapes. My profile is to the mirrors, and I am talking to someone about nothing important. I turn to face a mirror, a medium-sized square one. I see my face full on, and it turns into my mother's face bit by bit: cheekbones, eyes, chin. I quickly look away. I look into a different mirror and my face is my own. I don't usually look like my mother, I think. Then I step back to face the first mirror, and my face again turns into my mother's. I turn my back to the mirror and find myself looking out the familiar French doors and wrought-iron balcony of my childhood living room on the fifth floor. It is night. And there is my mother, with huge angel's wings, flying outside the doors. She waves and smiles.

I am in my kitchen, in reality the New York City kitchen of my childhood, with dark wood cabinets and variegated white laminate countertops. My mother is there, cleaning and organising. She is helping me as she helped me with the dishes and laundry in my Cheverly kitchen after Isaac was born. She is talking with me, but I cannot remember what she says, except one thing: I ask her what other people would hear if they walked in on our conversation. Would they be able to hear her? As she wipes down the counter, she says I would appear to be talking to myself, carrying on both sides of the conversation. I pop in and out of the kitchen and peer up the long hallway to make sure no one is coming.

When I cleaned out the New York City flat, I found a piece of the kitchen countertop in my old bedroom closet. It was the piece cut out to make way for the sink, rectangular with rounded edges. When I was a child, my mother would pull it out when I was doing anything messy, such as painting, so the mess was contained. She saved it all these years for if and when I had children. I brought it home for Isaac, who pulls it out himself when he wants to paint or use modelling clay.

WHEN MY MOTHER went back home to Sydney, I started calling the hollow tree 'Grandma's tree' so Isaac would think of her each time we went to the playground. He insisted on stopping at it whenever we walked past and noted it even from the car window if we were driving along that street. 'Look, Grandma's tree!' he'd shout and point.

I try, but don't always remember to take something from home to put in it. I've had to search my handbag for anything—a coin even—when I have come out unprepared. And like my mother, I have to be quick, sly. As he has grown, Isaac watches my every move more closely, and he is ready for the tree, looking toward it well before we reach it.

On her last visit, in the down time between her chemotherapy treatments, my mother often felt ill and took many naps. She was not up to taking Isaac to the playground. One afternoon, however, she went out for a walk by herself. She asked me which dinosaur she should take. I handed her a little blue Tyrannosaurus Rex. She left it in the hollow of the tree for Isaac to find later. When we walked by the tree the next day, and Isaac stopped and peered in, he jumped. Maybe my sleight of hand had become obvious to a three-year-old's eyes. He still enjoyed looking into the tree, but it was now routine, and he probably knew I was the culprit, the source of the treasures found in the hollow. But this find was magic.

Champagne, Cemeteries and Curls

ARABELLA EDGE

MOST SUMMERS AS A CHILD, I would fly from London to Glasgow where my grandmother lived in a tall narrow house with steep stone steps leading down to the street, Kingussie Drive. I travelled first class because I classified as a minor.

One time when I was ten, my mother packed six half bottles of Moët & Chandon in my bags, wrapping them among my clothes so that they wouldn't clink and break on the journey. Sitting by the window, my luggage carefully stowed in the overhead locker, I thought of the champagne nestled in my skirts and jumpers and felt a rush of excitement, that I should be the bearer of such a refined and sophisticated gift. I glanced at the air stewardess sashaying along the aisle, her glossy black hair tied beneath a powder blue peaked hat, and longed for a cherry red lipstick just like hers. Soon I would be in my grandmother's bedroom, trying on her perfumes, her rouge and mascara.

When the taxi swung down the hill and pulled up at the gate, I tried to take my case from the driver but he marched up the steps two at a time and rang the bell. Mamiesmamie stood smiling at the doorway. She wore a kaftan of shimmering green and purple silk. The thin gown rippled against her legs in the breeze, and brushed her silver sandals knotted at the ankle.

When I stood on tiptoe to kiss her, she smelled of gardenias and her thick loose blonde hair swung across my face as she leaned forward to hug me. She too made a move towards my luggage, but I gripped the handles and managed to carry my bags through the hallway where I glimpsed a door half open and then close.

My grandmother lived with her brother Billy. Mamiesmamie occupied the front parlour overlooking the scarlet geraniums and pinks spilling down the drive, and my great-uncle the back room. Between them lay the dining room, a dark mahogany-furnished interior in which Billy took his meals and where my grandmother never ate. Her bedroom faced the street and his the rambling, ragged stretch of lawn behind the house. The small, wood-panelled spare room where I would sleep had become a silent buffer between them, as if by unspoken consent they had divided the house vertically from attic to porch—the upstairs bathroom and ground floor kitchen, their only territory of uneasy truce.

For eleven years, Mamiesmamie and Billy had co-existed like this and in that time had barely exchanged a word. All I knew from my grandmother was that Billy had lied about his age and enlisted in the cavalry at sixteen, 'a foolish boy craving adventure'. I had been shown his tarnished medals, and had touched the frayed, worn ribbons, powdery with a scent of mothballs and dust. I had seen and admired a faded photograph of him in full uniform, proud and upright in the saddle, holding the reins tight on an alert, arched-necked bay stallion.

From an early age, I had been informed in hushed whispers that Billy did not like small children who made a noise, that I must tiptoe about and never bang doors, that when he returned from the trenches to this same house to live with his mother—Ma, my great-grandmother who, in her last months, Mamiesmamie had rushed from London to nurse—she soon learned to remove the whistle from the kettle because he could no longer endure its piercing shriek.

My grandmother ushered me into the parlour. Water-colours, still lifes, sketches and portraits of my mother and her cousins crammed the walls; the shelves were lined with books and busts of a slender, high cheek-boned negress who had posed in her sculpture class. I sat in my favourite place, the cane rocking chair framed by a gilt-edged glass screen salvaged from a Knightsbridge tearoom before the wreckers moved in.

Mamiesmamie disappeared into the kitchen and returned with a jug of elderflower water and a plate of egg and cress sandwiches. She reclined on a velvet chaise longue, lit a Sobranie cigarette and watched with pleasure as I ate.

'Extraordinary to think,' she began, exhaling plumes of smoke, golden shafts in the late afternoon light, 'that everything from the Maida Vale apartment fitted into this place.'

The house in Kingussie Drive represented her exile from Lanark Road in Little Venice to Glasgow, and despite the years she'd been there, in her entire lifetime it would never truly become her home.

She paused at a hesitant shuffling sound in the hallway, the familiar faltering, slippered tread.

'Off to the pub again.'

We waited for the front door to swing shut. Mamiesmamie flicked open the net curtains and gazed out at the stooped, retreating form.

'How he makes it up and down the steps, God only knows.'

I clicked open my case, or valise as my mother would have said when she gave it to me on my eighth birthday, a smart travelling bag, white creamy leather, pure pigskin.

I told my grandmother to close her eyes. Carefully I laid the bottles in a row on the carpet before the fireplace.

'You can look now,' I said.

'Oh my,' she exclaimed, her hands darting to smooth

her hair, as if the champagne represented formal and unexpected company. 'How wonderful of Marianne.'

She reached for another cigarette and peered about the room. 'The piano, of course,' my grandmother said. 'Thank God for the upright piano.'

She picked up two of the bottles and instructed me to go over and pull down the front panel between the pedals and keys.

'Sacrilege, I know,' she said. 'Don't tell your mother.'

Effortlessly at my touch, the wooden flap dropped open. She stood beside me, pinged a loud note and placed the champagne inside.

'Bring the others,' she whispered, thumping out the first chords of a tune. 'Sur Le Pont D'Avignon,' she sang, 'on y danse, on y danse.'

Later, once all was stowed away, we crept furtively upstairs.

'I have paper bags,' she confided, tucking me in. 'Boring ones from Woolworths—nothing that would interest him.' She nodded her head in the direction of Billy's room. 'I can hide the bottles in the fridge, one by one, behind the eggs and that ghastly cream whip you so enjoy.' She laughed softly to herself. 'Perhaps, now is the time,' she murmured.

When with a kiss, she tiptoed away, I snuggled in the crisp starched sheets, eager to re-enact my grandmother's plan in my mind.

Mamiesmamie had seized on the idea the summer before last. A matter of logistics, she confided. She had arrived here eleven years ago to nurse her ailing mother and now found herself trapped with a brother who refused to be budged. Any move would have to be accomplished by stealth.

It would depend on a good quart of whisky, she had said. Famous Grouse, to make the Christmas pudding, but which she would leave on the kitchen table in a forgetful way. Billy would not believe his luck. But first she had to grind the sleeping pills, a prescription my grandmother had obtained and never taken. Instead, the blue capsules were waiting for Billy and my grandmother's dramatic escape to our house in north London.

She would use Ma's wheelchair, still stacked at the end of my bed—I gazed at it fondly—and with my help, she would heave her unconscious brother onto the seat, call a cab to the station, and all three of us would take the sleeper to Euston, a double cabin for her and me, a single for Billy. I imagined lying in the top bunk above my grandmother, with the shutters up so that the dimming lights of the platforms flashed past, the darkening outlines of villages and church spires. How I loved to drift on this dream, drowsily shooing away the improbabilities, the potential flaws in Mamiesmamie's plot.

'What if he wakes up,' I once had asked, 'and finds himself on a train in the middle of the night. He might panic and pull the emergency cord.'

Mamiesmamie shook her head. 'Oh no, dear, those pills will knock him out.'

On another occasion, I suggested that perhaps it would be simpler just to leave him behind. Why not fly back to London with me instead?

At this, she darted me one of her looks, her eyebrow raised in distinct disapproval.

'I couldn't do that,' she retorted, clicking her tongue. 'He's my brother, after all. I'm all he's got.'

She lit a cigarette and thought for a while. 'Besides,' she said, 'I'm sure he'll enjoy himself, once he has recovered from the shock. You never know,' she glanced my way, 'the change might do him good.'

I suppose we both knew she would never leave Glasgow. Nevertheless, discussing the plan greatly amused her and I revelled in the excitement of this secret between us.

Most mornings, I sat with Billy in the gloom of the dining room, the heavy brocade curtains drawn against the harsh morning light. I had to concentrate over breakfast not to rattle the spoon in my teacup, bash open the soft-boiled egg, or butter my toast in a noisy fashion. I imagined myself a mouse, quiet and meek, chewing each mouthful with silent delicate jaws.

Yet two years ago when my ballet school had staged a performance of *The Pied Piper of Hamelin*, I had been a rat, a large powerful rat, sporting a thick nylon tail, black tights and a leotard, a painted mask with long whiskers and pointed ears. All the pretty girls had been waves, beautiful languid waves in blue satin gowns. They had lain side by side and, at Madame Vacarni's instructions, had lifted their slender arms in unison to the music tinkling from the piano.

But I had been decreed a rat. I was meant to scamper stage right at the sound of a fiddle and nibble on a bright yellow square of cardboard cheese. Before my mother, I cried and stormed. 'I want to be a wave,' I said.

My mother laughed. 'I will make sure,' she declared, 'that you will be a rat no one will ever forget.'

My mother stuck to her word. My rat costume was terrifying. All the silly little wave children screamed at my approach.

'Enter Carabosse,' I would cry, 'followed by her retinue of rats.' And I would hear the rousing roar of percussion and drums on my record of *Sleeping Beauty*.

Such was the success of my performance that the moment I came home from school, I would change into my costume.

However, Billy did not like the rat which, forgetting itself, had scampered into his dining room one morning the summer before last. Nor did he appreciate the creature crouching on the chair at the table, nor the shrill squeaks emitted from the rat mask and the horrible scrabbling claws, all of which I had rehearsed to perfection.

But even before Mamiesmamie was called to intervene, my life as a rat came to a terrible and demeaning end. Later that same day, I accidentally peed on the beautiful nylon tail and when, embarrassed, I finally explained what had happened, my grandmother discreetly threw the entire outfit away.

Always at breakfast Billy asked me two questions. 'How long are you staying this time?' he would enquire, peering from behind his newspaper, which he held before his face as a barrier against the unwelcome intrusion in the room where for decades he had taken his meals alone.

At my reply, he would stare in silence at some article he was pretending to read. Then once again, the paper would be lowered.

'And when are you going home?'

I remember one rainy summer reading a Tarzan novel in bed—Mamiesmamie sometimes insisted on afternoon rests—and I heard a sound of singing from the garden: mournful, elegiac, drifting through the open window, carried by a breeze billowing the net curtains. I peeked outside. Billy was raking leaves from the lawn and piling them onto a smouldering damp fire. He wore a tweed hat, beige coat and bore a striking resemblance to Paddington Bear as he warbled in a sweet, wavering voice the half-remembered refrains of music hall songs he had heard before the war.

'Pale hands I loved beside the Shalimar …'
'Little Dolly Daydream, tra la la …'

After breakfast, Mamiesmamie and I usually had the house to ourselves. Billy would take himself off to the local lending library to leaf through old copies of *Punch* before pub opening time.

The morning after I arrived, that summer I was ten, I lounged by the open door in the kitchen watching Mamiesmamie make scones for afternoon tea. The moment she heard Billy shuffle past, she tucked one of the bottles of champagne, quickly wrapped in dowdy brown paper, between a sponge cake and a tub of cream at the back of the fridge.

She whistled as she bustled about. She'd tied her hair in a red bandana, which gave her a raffish look. She glanced at the clock.

'Oh my,' she cried, 'it can't be twelve already. There's a recording of *Fingal's Cave* on the radio. I'd hate to miss it. Quick, bring the champagne and we'll sit in the parlour.'

Ceremoniously I carried the chilled bottle along the hallway. Mamiesmamie had switched on the radio and a solemn BBC voice echoed from the speaker. She motioned me to the cane rocking chair as she unlocked the walnut cabinet, chose two green, long-stemmed cut-crystal glasses, and set them on the table between us. I was allowed to unpeel the golden foil and twist away the wire. Then my grandmother popped the cork with an expert hand.

'Music to my ears,' she declared and filled each flute to the foaming brim.

So entranced was I by the spectacle, that I forgot to ask who she might be expecting. All at once, a crescendo of violins filled the room.

'Ah, Mendelssohn,' she sighed, and lifted her glass. 'To your good health, my darling.'

I stared at her watching, waiting expression. Clearly I was meant to do something.

'I've always been a firm believer,' she announced, 'in champagne being drunk at any age and at any time.'

Hesitantly, I reached out. Mamiesmamie leaned forward and clinked her glass against mine.

On occasions, with Charlie, my grandfather, her ex-husband in France, I had been allowed wine and water, a bitter diluted concoction the colour of Ribena. But this … I took a sip and felt the ice-cold bubbles burst on my lips and tongue, savoured the magical elixir I had smuggled all the way from London and that Mamiesmamie and I had secreted away right under old Uncle Billy's sharp, knowing eyes.

My grandmother lit a Sobranie. 'Now I'm in absolute heaven,' she breathed. She stretched out on the chaise longue.

I waited for the first movement of *Fingal's Cave* to die away.

'Tell me about Charlie,' I begged.

How I loved her to reminisce about my grandfather—glamorous, sophisticated Charlie with his seductive French accent and its undertow of German, he of the Saville Row suits and camel hair jackets, coats lined in wolf fur, shoes of the softest leather, a solid gold cigarette case and slender ivory filter, silk shirts and cashmere sweaters ordered from Harrods, and of citrus cologne, Moustache, which mingled with his musk scent of expensive tobacco, a mix of Virginian and Russian. Charlie, who was now driving Tilly, his current mistress, to Cassis in an open-topped Rolls Royce.

'Oh, it was such a long time ago,' Mamiesmamie would say as she sipped her champagne.

Yet she enjoyed talking about the past, her first and only love, the whirlwind romance at the age of nineteen with the impeccably mannered French engineer who whisked her away from the confines of Kingussie Drive to his family estate, the ornamental lakes and landscaped grounds of Vernon in northern France. She did not tell me then about her syphilitic father-in-law and his two whores, or about Charlie's long absences and the assignations with his tubercular mother's nurse; all this I would learn later.

'There were tea dances at the Plaza where a band played the Black Bottom and the Charleston,' Mamiesmamie would begin in a dreamy voice.

It was as if I weren't there, a ten-year-old child, her grand-daughter seated quietly before her, taking furtive, exquisite gulps from a crystal glass clasped tightly in my clumsy hand.

SOMETIMES BUT NOT OFTEN, during the school holidays I would be dispatched on the express train from Euston to Coventry. Granny Edge lived on the outskirts of town in a severe pebble-dashed semi-detached overlooking the M4 motorway. Even inside, with the windows shut tight and the doors firmly locked, you could never escape the constant roar of the traffic. At night, in the stifling room where I slept, a sulphur yellow light from the street lamps glowed through the chintz curtains and only a faint glimmer of stars could be seen in the night skies.

Granny Edge only wore her teeth for special company and when she fetched me from the station, would press her gummy mouth so fiercely against my cheek that it left a red mark.

'My, your hair is in a right frizz,' she would say, inspecting me from top to toe as we waited at the bus stop. And taking an elastic band from her coat pocket, she would try to twist my unruly tangles into the semblance of a ponytail.

For as long as I could remember, my grandfather lay supine like an ancient beached turtle on a huge floral upholstered sofa, his head propped on innumerable cushions. According to my grandmother, he suffered in summer from prickly heat, which explained his white singlets, which strained like netting against his soft white corpulent flesh. Every so often Granny Edge would dart towards him and dust him with puffs of talcum powder as if he were a slab of suet to be kneaded in flour. If Granny Edge was lean and raw-boned, veins protruding like sinews from her arms and scraggy neck, he was like a giant sea mammal, invertebrate, craving another element. I imagined him set free at last, floating above a silent sand floor, ribbed by the tides, hearing great gusts expelled from his lungs, the twitch and flicker of a jet black tail, his pale mournful squid eyes peering through darkening forests of kelp.

Clicking her tongue in a toothless mouth, my grandmother would bring out endless trays of food—meat loaf, cottage pie, steak piled with chips and sauce. My grandfather had little choice but to eat it all. In this cramped sitting room, he could not move, his legs weighed down with quilts and rugs. And I too felt oppressed by the large rose patterns scrolling the wallpaper, the florid matching curtains, the overstuffed armchairs fitted with antimacassars, the quilted pouffes on either side of the fireplace, the mock Jacobean dresser in which Granny kept her best china, the collection of Toby jugs arranged neatly on a shelf.

From the moment my parents became engaged, Granny Edge never approved of my mother. Why, at thirty-five, she was ten years older than her only son—and insolent too, with her fancy French ways.

'Before our John started seeing that woman,' I once heard my grandmother say, 'he always took three spoons of sugar in his tea.'

My parents met on a P&O liner voyaging to Australia; he was a headwaiter and she the ship's nanny. Bored on deck during her odd hours off duty, my mother was attracted to my father's sun-bleached hair and ready smile, the starched white uniform which showed off his tan. And he found himself bedazzled by this sophisticated woman who recently had lived in an apartment with views of the Eiffel Tower.

After I had kissed my grandfather on the forehead and Granny Edge had retreated to the kitchen, I would kneel before the tall glass cabinet, crammed with the souvenirs my father had sent home—carved ebony elephants from Ceylon, their ivory tusks tipped with gold; silks from Singapore; satin slippers from Hong Kong; various jade figurines; alabaster chess pieces; ship menus; thick embossed cards illustrated with sulphur-crested cockatoos, lorikeets and rosellas, their brilliant plumage as impossibly exotic as the tale of the firebird.

'Don't touch,' Granny would say, jerking her head through the servery hatch if my hand strayed towards the key. 'They're our John's.'

Having exhausted the possibilities of Granny's souvenir cabinet, sometimes I was allowed to read the menus—prawn cocktail, lobster bisque, grilled Dover sole, bombe Alaska. My grandfather would ask me to put a record on the gramophone from his vast collection of Gilbert & Sullivan. I would choose his favourites—*The Gondoliers, HMS Pinafore*. He liked the volume turned up and would close his eyes, tapping his fingers, anticipating the tempo.

He had a passion for music, and Shakespeare, could recite the sonnets by heart. And when he did, I would sit on a stool by the sofa, enthralled by his low sonorous voice.

From you have I been absent in the spring
When proud-pied April, dress'd in all his trim,
Hath put a spirit of youth in everything,
That heavy Saturn laugh'd and leapt with him.

As he spoke, relishing every word and rhythm, the busy clatter in the kitchen would cease. Not a sound. Granny too was listening through the half-open hatch of the servery.

'And the one about the lilies,' I would ask.

He would gaze down at me and smile. 'You like the dark ones, don't you?' And clearing his throat, he would begin:

The summer's flower is to the summer sweet,
Though to itself it only live and die;
But if that flower with base infection meet,
The basest weed outbraves its dignity:
For sweetest things turn sourest by their deeds;
Lilies that fester smell far worse than weeds.

Most mornings, my grandmother would propose an outing. By the way she glanced at me, I'd know exactly what it would be.

'Let's visit our Uncle Jack.'

Directly opposite the house, across the busy motorway, lay the cemetery. The tombs ranged in rows against raw parklands surrounded by ploughed meadows. As the cars and lorries streaked past, Granny Edge would take my hand in hers. If I dawdled or forgot to keep pace, she'd rub my knuckles so hard beneath her strong grip that I thought my bones would crack.

She marched me along the mown grass paths between the graves, tutting at the neglected headstones matted with briars and weeds until we reached the neat, turfed mound beneath which resided her long-dead brother. Uncle Jack, born deaf and dumb, my grandmother's favourite, the only brother who could not enlist in the war.

As we stood side by side, I would glance up at Granny, her expression stern and unforgiving beneath her wide-brimmed hat. Year in, year out, she tended this plot. Sighing, she would unlock the wooden crate in which she kept her broom, her trowel, the watering can, and proceed to sweep the swathes of dead leaves which had gathered against the black granite plinth.

'Before the funeral I chose and paid for that,' she'd announce, snatching a cloth and wiping the stark gilt lettering.

Jack William Bates. Dearly departed, 1899–1918 —
Taken away by the flu pandemic.

'Nursed him myself, I did,' she'd mutter under her breath.

And itching in the scratchy jumper and skirt she'd knitted, I'd gaze out at the fields far beyond where ripening thickets of blackberries tangled the hedgerows, and I imagined myself a boy, a cheery sturdy boy, with cornflower blue eyes and a fox hound at my heels.

Granny would take my hand in hers, gently this time. 'Come on, Jack,' she'd say. 'Let's go brambling.'

On the few mornings when it was too wet or windy to visit the cemetery, my grandmother would crimp my hair with a pair of hot iron tongs in the fashion of her day, when she was a young woman. She gave me a side parting and styled the stiff curls into a series of waves pinned at the nape of my neck. Inspecting my reflection in the mirror, I'd see someone I barely recognised, hair scraped back from a pale expressionless face, as if I too were a distant memory, a faded image on a Daguerreotype plate.

Sometimes, sitting patiently while she artfully rearranged my hair, or watching my grandmother kneel by her brother's grave in the heat and the dust, the mud and the rain, rearranging the plastic roses and carnations in a stained brown vase, a tremendous sadness would fill me, a sadness for something I did not know and would never understand.

Merit Card

SARA DOWSE

THE SUNLIGHT HAS FADED IT, but on my fridge door is a document of great consequence, and I can't bring myself to remove it. Not yet. Not for a while. For this is my merit card, my great treasure, and surely the only one of its kind. One side, the side that hasn't yet faded, is covered with stickers of infantilised animals: baby pandas, dinosaurs, pigs, bunnies, turtles, and the like, all anthropomorphised and drawn in the ghastly psychedelic colours that toy manufacturers nowadays seem to delight in, as though preparing their young customers for a lifetime of addiction to hallucinatory drugs. This is the side quite properly facing the door. But on the other side, the side that matters and that the sun will soon leach of any decipherable meaning, is the inscription: *Grandma Dowse for beying a really really good grandma*. Done in red ink, no less, as if to emphasise the point.

The author of this cherished citation is Grace Ella Dowse, aged six as I write, the daughter of my third son Josh. For quite a long while Grace looked a lot like me. I'd look at her baby pictures and photos of an infant me and, overlooking the scratches on mine, they could have been of the same person. Same black hair, same dark eyes. But now this is changing; Grace has evolved as her own inimitable self. The dark eyes remain, but the hair is lighter, thick but straight, and hangs right down to her waist. She is a bright yet nervy child, but at least God has spared her my curls.

Grace lives with her father and mother, Sarah, two older brothers, Tom and Barney, and a baby sister, Eve, in the same Sydney suburb as I do now. She strives to keep up with her brothers, and tries to dominate her sister. Not only is she surrounded by siblings, her whole life has been cushioned by cousins, a good deal from her mother's side of the family and quite a few from mine. Although cushioned, perhaps, is quite the wrong word. Grace is the child of a huge family, and families like hers are microcosms of the world.

It was kind of Grace to think of me when she wrote out my merit card—inspired, I should say, from the many she's received herself—but it has underscored a niggling feeling of mine that I'm really not as good as it says. Every time I open the fridge I'm reminded of my failings. I look after Grace and her sister more than my other grandchildren because they live so close, but it's still not much. I hear of other grandmothers who regularly look after their grandchildren, who bring them little presents and have them spend the night. Not just occasionally but one or two times a week. Or others who pick them up from school, or act as full-time childminders for their parents. I do baby-sit almost whenever I'm asked, but my children are careful not to ask too often. It's as though at last, after all these years, they've come to respect what I do with my time.

The truth of it is that I may not have been much chop as a mother either, but perhaps in both cases—parenting and grandparenting—my shortcomings have resulted less from any deficiency of affection as from an excess of progeny. A couple of blocks from where I'm living now is the house where we lived when my first four kids were young, and a block or two in the other direction lived a woman who became my best friend. Together we muddled through our days. One afternoon while our kids were rushing around she turned to me and said, 'You know, some women think of this as a job.' What an extraordinary statement, I thought; so much so I had to ask her what she meant. 'Just what I said,' she answered. 'They think of it as a job.'

I didn't get it then and get it even less today. To some extent, my kids and I led parallel lives. At least that's how I saw it. I was there to nurture and protect them, but

I wasn't interested in shaping them. For this strange attitude I have to go back to my own childhood, I guess, informed as it was by what today we might call benign neglect. Nor did my being a migrant help. I never understood why in the stratified world of 1960s Sydney it was considered important to send one's kids to private schools, and was amazed to learn that a conscientious parent would sign up a child at birth. I was shocked at the competitiveness too. If my boys wanted to play sport, well and good, but I was damned if I was going to stand on the sidelines and yell at them to perform. If my daughter wanted to wear dresses with as many ruffles as they could carry, that was fine, but she couldn't expect me to iron them. I hated fights between the two oldest boys and could be ruthless in suppressing them, but most of the time I let them be. It was enough to just get through the washing and the cleaning and the shopping and the cooking and then, and only then, get on with my own life. So it shouldn't be surprising that I let them get on with theirs.

It's a truism, I suppose, that the fewer children one has the more attention each one of them gets, and the same must hold for grandchildren. Otherwise you're in danger of choosing favourites. If my laissez-faire approach to parenting had its pitfalls, favouritism wasn't one of them. I was able to love my children equally and still be sensitive to each of their special qualities. Because I opened this piece with Grace, you might suppose that now I'm a grandparent I've said goodbye to the qualms I once had about favouring one child over another, but the fact is that my egalitarian spirit is as strong as ever, and what I do love about each of my grandchildren is that he or she already has a story. I couldn't claim to know any of them entirely, each of them (like all human beings, most of all myself) remains something of a mystery; yet still, for a writer, stories are the greatest hook on earth. I fell in love with my husband because he told such fabulous stories about London during the Blitz and mountaineering and living in the wild, and my grandchildren have proved equally beguiling. Take Grace's sister Eve who, aged two, has assigned each family member and even the most casual acquaintance with an animal persona. That's what I mean about mysteries—where did a two-year-old find the genius to do that?

My oldest grandchild, Jasper, is an adolescent now, and these days I am, understandably, very much on the periphery of his life. When I recall myself at his age, however, I remember wanting to live with my grandmother. She was kind, kinder than my parents, I thought, and her flat wasn't far from my school. Through pestering my mother I did succeed in staying with her a few months, until being responsible for the fey, inconsiderate flatmate that I was proved too much for her to handle. She was much younger than I am now but had a dicky heart and I was too wrapped up in my adolescent dreams to take that fully into account. She died not long after I migrated to Australia, and her death was very painful for me. In those days you didn't travel back and forth like you can now, and in any case I hardly had the money.

But a few years after Jasper was born I decided to go back to North America. It was Canada I went to, not the US, but for a time I thought I could close the circle by returning, more or less, to my roots. And I did reconnect with a lot of my American family and many old childhood friends. I flew back and forth to Australia each year but it wasn't enough. The pull was too strong. The matter was clinched when my daughter warned, 'If you don't come back, Mum, your grandchildren won't even know who you are.' Her remark hit home, but much more sobering than that was my realising how much I was missing by not knowing who they were.

I was present at Jasper's birth, which was a wonderful gift, but almost from the start he was ambivalent about me. He twigged early on that whenever I walked in the door his mother was walking out. Unlike my own kids, Jasper was demand fed and from my somewhat jaundiced perspective was hugely attached to his mother. I think his first words were 'No grandma'. I laugh at that to this day, but underneath it hurt. How did one lure a child from his all-embracing mother? Eventually he succumbed to my cuddles but then I went off to Canada. One day on a visit back to Australia I went to his school, something that grandparents were—and I imagine still are—encouraged to do. I expected that I would be asked to read a story, or tell the children something about my peripatetic life.

Instead I was nakedly commandeered to help the children with their work. One poor seven-year-old will never escape the ignominy of having been led astray with his maths. Nor will Jasper or I. But I look forward to the day when teachers have the resources to do their job without coopting grandparents.

Now that Jasper's a teenager and communicates in grunts there's little I can help him with except to be there for him, but there was a time when my long-ago experience of being the child of divorce was of use. We were in the car and his younger sister Han taunted him, as children cruelly do, for not having the same father as she does. Jasper's eyes clouded with tears—not because he doesn't love his father but due to that all-encompassing need of children to be like everyone else. Having felt the same thing myself once, I was able to tell Hannah what she was doing wrong and saw Jasper's relief and surprise that his grandmother understood.

Unlike their academic cousins in my part of the city, I suspect that both Hannah and Jasper are the kind of kids whose apparent 'underachievement' indicates true talent: a floundering in a sea of dull, conformist schooling that all too often is unable to accommodate it. I think of Isaac Babel, who read novels on his music stand while pretending to play the violin, or my own brother, who dropped out of school to become a motorcycle mechanic and ended up designing rockets for NASA, or the many friends and acquaintances of mine who, despite merely adequate academic performance—or less—have shone in later life.

In certain ways, Hannah and Jasper already have. The children of artist fathers, they are both outstanding artists themselves and impressive lateral thinkers. Last summer my daughter Jess and her husband Matt took the kids to the stage edition of the popular television show *Spicks and Specks*, chiefly because of Matt's extensive knowledge of popular music. So when Adam Hills asked for volunteers from the audience, Han shot up her hand and pointed proudly to her father. But to her surprise and great secret pleasure she, aged nine, was chosen herself. She sat on the stage with the adults and acquitted herself with such aplomb that Adam Hills slid to his knees and exclaimed, 'Hannah, we aren't worthy of you. You are the coolest person I have ever met.' And he's right.

Hannah might have her mother's savvy and great looks, but the person she looks up to most in the universe is her older cousin Georgie, my second eldest grandchild and possibly the one I see least. Georgie lives on the other side of Sydney, with her mother. Her parents, like Jasper's, split up early in her life. That, of course, is her story, and she's dealt with it by being almost resolutely cheerful, in any case in my presence, and developing a powerful sense of justice. Now that she, too, is in her teens, she's begun to ask questions, and it's interesting that the person she's directed them to is me. A big responsibility, and an honour, that. Her father Jake, my second eldest son, has remarried and he and Lu have produced Reg and Arkie, two most singular children. Reg is a beautiful boy, sensitive yet totally bohemian in his attitude to the world, if that's the right term for an eight-year-old, and I often ponder how he's going to manage when all the many pressures to conform come to impact on him.

His sister Arkie climbs anything and everything and likes to run away. I had to chase after her around the circumference of Trumper Oval one day when I was minding her and she raced out the door. She's a devil—there's no other way to put it—and drives her mother mad. Well, children can do that, let's not pretend. At one time or other each of my grandchildren has taken the mickey out of me, and I've got a revenge of sorts by casually referring to them as bandits to their doting parents. Especially Barney and Tom. Each on their own commendably respectful, the two together used to put me through hell, taking the house apart when their parents were out, climbing in and out of their beds. According to their mother, Barney, shyer than he lets on, used to be frightened by the shadow my hair cast on the wall. Now he has big hair himself. Now they no longer torment me, or anyone else for that matter. The two little demons have grown into fine, considerate boys, and as Germaine Greer has written there's nothing quite so beautiful as a nine-year-old boy, give or take a year. Anyway, before they become teenagers and the scourge of their parents' lives. Tom, who called me 'mine friend Grandma' when he was very young, has gone through much of that already, and I suspect has calmed down for good.

Now that I've taken you on a journey around my nine grandchildren, I hope I've succeeded in giving you an idea of their separate selves. To me, anyway, that's the most important thing about them. The very fact that all are healthy and bright and beautiful—if I may say so, but it's true—I consider an enormous blessing. Do I want to be treated like a grand matriarch and have them quake at the sight of me? The very idea makes me laugh, just as, sometimes, my being a mother did. Here I was, a girl who spurned dolls and never learned to cook, the mother of five, so who could have dreamt that I'd become a grandmother? There's that thing about immortality, the wondrous notion that every grandchild carries a bit of us in them and is shaped in ways they could never know by our pasts. But to me it's their mortality, not my immortality that matters. What matters is what I see before me now, and the changes I'm privileged to witness. How their stories evolve.

One day they will write their stories themselves, if not on paper then on some electronic device or even just in their heads. And their grandmother's limited perspective might prod them to refute what I've written or, if I'm lucky, help them gain some further insight into themselves. As for their future, frankly it scares me. How are these nine grand people going to cope with the disasters predicted for them? There's not much that makes me angry these days, but the fact that my children and their children are likely to suffer because of my generation's greed and my own good fortune makes me both angry and ashamed.

Every time I hear a politician oppose action on climate change lest it should ruin the economy, or make political capital out of the high price of petrol, I'm angry. Every time I see a McMansion or an SUV or most of the ads in the newspapers, I'm choked with anger. I'm angry at the unwillingness of people to make sacrifices and the politicians who won't risk asking them to. I'm angry with the governments that sat on the crest of a boom and wrapped Sydney up with motorways and tunnels instead of improving our public transport and encouraging people to use it. I wonder what will happen when Australia runs out of water. I think of Grace, and her merit card, and I fear that none of us have been the grandparents her generation deserves.

Bread and Lemons

MICHELE DI'BARTOLO

MARIA SAMPERI HOLDS the ends of her shawl in a fist that she has placed firmly in the centre of her chest. Covering her head and secured by a tight knot beneath her chin, is a plain scarf. It keeps her long mane of plaited dark hair and small head covered, but it gives little comfort and no protection against the winds that are tearing at the eastern coast of Sicily. This triangle-shaped island is caught between the toe of Italy and the rim of North Africa, trapped between two great forces and held aloft by the currents of opposing seas. And on this dark night in 1930, it also sits at the centre of a tempest.

Maria Samperi takes an even tighter hold of her shawl and offers up a silent prayer to Santa Barbara, the patron saint of bad weather.

But there is no wind that will turn her back tonight.

There is only going on until she has found what it is that she is looking for.

The cart she's sitting on rolls forward.

I PASS MY FATHER a loaf of Italian bread. It's Sunday and as always, my family is gathered around the table for our traditional weekly fare. With quick fingers and one well-practised move, my father pulls a hunk of bread away from the body of the loaf.

'Do you want a knife?' I ask and hold one out, the brown handle pointed towards him.

He just shakes his head.

'Bread tastes better when you pull it apart with your hands,' he says.

I put my knife down.

'I've never heard that before.'

This time my father nods and his eyes, in that shade of startling blue that runs through his family tree, are bright.

'That's what my grandmother always said. She never put a knife to a loaf of bread.'

My father passes back the loaf. I look at it and turn it over in my hands.

THE WHEELS of the cart slow down and the donkey whines in relief.

'Signora Maria,' the man at the front of the cart says, looking back at his small, female passenger. His voice is tired and the wind has been battering at him for hours now. 'We can't go on tonight, not in this weather.'

She looks up at him, her blue eyes brilliant in the night.

'We find him tonight,' she says simply as the wind tries to pick loose the knot beneath her chin, 'we find him tonight.'

The driver reaches up to readjust his cap and Maria reaches for her bag. She pulls out a loaf of bread and breaks a piece off with strong, thin fingers. Maria hands the piece of bread to the driver who takes it without lifting his eyes from her face. She just looks away and out into the night, her shawl and scarf tight around her tiny body.

Maria Samperi stands at just a scratch under five feet tall and on a heavy day she tips the scale at forty kilos. If not for the steel core holding her firmly to earth, the night's wind would pick her up and take her with it, across the island of Sicily and out to Africa.

The driver sighs but does not attempt to change her mind. Instead he just turns, urges the donkey on and bites down hard on his piece of bread.

'NONNA MARIA made her own bread,' my father says.

Once a week she'd get up at 2 am. She'd mix the dough, knead it and bake it in an old bread oven. She'd bake enough for all her children and their families to last them an entire week.

My father sighs. 'And then when she was done baking, she'd get ready and go to work.'

MARIA SAMPERI has a lot of time on her journey to think. She is travelling a long way from the village she calls home and there's not much to see along the way. The Sicilian landscape of 1930 is rocky and dark and the sound of the wind and her prayers block out all other sound. She releases the ends of her shawl for a moment so she can rub her hands together. Her skin, thanks to the lemons, is tight and thin. Grooves are starting to appear across her knuckles and the tips of her fingers where the acid has started to find its way in. Maria pulls her shawl tight again and closes her eyes.

In the darkness she can see colour.

The yellow of the lemons with which she spends her days.

In the darkness she can smell them.

Their acidic cloud winds itself around her head and beneath her she can feel the shape of the wicker stool on which she sits and works six days a week. Every day, that is, except Sunday because that's the day of rest and of lunch.

'WHAT DID SHE DO in the groves?' I ask my father.

'In Sicilian,' he explains, 'she was called the *tagghiapeddi*, the lemon cutter. What you have to understand, is that in her day in Sicily, lemons were worth more than gold.' He takes a quick breath in. 'Each lemon was so precious and worth so much money that they had to be shipped out in perfect condition. You have to imagine,' my father goes on, 'that the pickers weren't allowed to bring down a single fruit from the tree, until the dew on them had dried. They had to be unmarked,' he says, 'and when they picked them they cut them from the tree with the stem still attached. Then they'd wrap each one in paper and take them up to my grandmother who was sitting in the barn waiting for them. I remember going up and seeing her, dressed all in black and surrounded by lemons. She'd unwrap each one, trim the stem down to the right height and send them off to be packed.'

From the rocky island and from my great-grandmother's peasant hands, these brilliant yellow gems were shipped around the world. They found their way to mainland Italy, across Europe to as far away as Russia and even across the ocean to America. And the one woman the lemon grove owners could trust above all others, to trim and polish and wrap them was my great-grandmother, Maria Samperi. A woman who had never seen, and never would, all the places her lemons went.

'How long did she work for?' I ask my father.

'Until she was eighty,' he replies, 'from when her husband ran off until she was eighty years old.'

'Did she ever find him?'

My father nods. 'She found him. In a little village further north along the coast.'

THE CART keeps heading north. Maria Samperi was born just before the legendary earthquake that broke the back and swallowed whole the ancient city of Messina. She is heading that way now, past the volcano whose shadow she was born in and towards the mainland she has never seen. Her eyes are still closed, her mind still adrift.

'Signora Maria!'

She hears the voice of the foreman who collects her for work every morning when it's still dark.

'Signora Maria!'

Signore Ucciardello, the lemon grove foreman, pulls up outside the timber door of her tiny stone house on his bicycle.

She appears every morning with her head scarf already in place and her dark shawl drawn tightly across her shoulders. Her long, dark skirt sweeps the rough ground as she pulls the front door closed, her two children still asleep inside. Maria takes a handful of skirt, lifts a leg and takes a seat between the handlebars of Signore Ucciardello's bicycle. She's no bigger than a child. And like that, every morning, she catches her lift to work.

In the dark and with the cold, they ride over rocky, dusty roads to where the stone houses of the village melt away and the iron gates of the lemon grove appear. There she heads to the barn where she takes up her seat and waits for the lemons.

'Signora Maria!'

Someone calls her name again but it's out of place in her mental wanderings. She opens her eyes and looks to the driver. The cart, she notices, has stopped on a tight road between two rows of stone houses.

'This is it, Signora Maria,' the driver says.

She looks around. The village is small, smaller even than the one she's come from. They have travelled so far north now that the volcano, usually so prominent in the sky, can no longer be seen or its overbearing presence felt. Only the wind fills the early hours of the morning and the heavy smell of rain weighs down the air.

But it's the perfect time to confront her wayward husband. It's the one hour she knows he'll be up. It's the bread-making hour.

'HIS NAME WAS MARIO,' my father says, 'no wait!' He holds up an elegant hand of thin, agile fingers. 'It was Nino!' He stops again and shakes his head. 'No, no, I'm pretty sure it was Mario.'

Before her twentieth birthday, Maria Samperi was married to a baker whose surname was Marino but whose first name seems, over time, to have been forgotten.

One day in 1930, Mario Marino, the baker, hit the dusty Sicilian road and didn't look back. His reasons for abandoning his family were known only to him because he left no note, no forwarding address, no rhyme or reason for his disappearance into the dark hills of Sicily. What he left behind was my great-grandmother, Maria Samperi, with two infant children and no means by which she could feed and keep them in their tiny stone house. The baker's wandering act came as a catastrophic blow; 1930s Sicily was no time for a woman to be left on her own.

It is no wonder then, that on returning home from the lemon groves not long after her husband's disappearance, and hearing news that the baker had been sighted further north, Maria Samperi arranged a driver and cart to brave a storm and hunt him down.

'I remember on the nights when it stormed and the doors and windows would shake,' my father says. 'Nonna Maria would spend the whole night praying to Santa Barbara.'

A constant chant to her most relied upon patron saint because, it turns out, there was nothing Maria Samperi feared more than a storm.

AS MARIA steps off the cart, the first drops of rain start to fall.

'Santa Barbara, look over me,' she whispers.

The ends of her shawl are now in a death grip in her little fist. She takes a few small steps and heads towards the village bakery.

'WHAT HAPPENED?' I ask my father.

He shakes his head and turns his palms upwards.

'I don't know,' he says, 'she never told me exactly what happened when she found him.'

That encounter, forever untold, now lies lost in the folds of my family's history.

'Did he go back with her?'

'No,' my father says, 'I know she found him in the bakery that morning, and they spent almost a year together in that town with their children. But then she woke up one morning and he was gone again.'

'She went back home alone?'

'Not quite,' my father says. 'She went back pregnant with their third child.'

THE SUN IS UP, the storm has long since passed and, betrayed by the baker for the final time, Maria Samperi steps back onto a cart. This time the donkey is facing the way she came. Soon, three sets of eyes will look to her for survival and all she has to feed them with are lemons.

By the time she gets back home from this village in the north, the lemon season will start to change and a different type of lemon will be grown. Not the precious kind that's to be trimmed and wrapped in paper, but a far sturdier variety. So too will her job change and she'll take up a new role in the production line. The lemons will still be delivered to her by the basket load but not with the same care as before. They'll be dumped all around her and with another set of quick, expert motions, she'll core each lemon and throw their skins into an enormous vat of lime. From the cored flesh of the lemon they'll make lemonade, but the skins, when melted down, will be shipped to North Italy to be used for perfume. Where the previous season's lemons took off only a thin layer of skin, the next batch will bleed acid streams and carve deep, burning wounds across her young hands.

Maria draws her shawl around herself again and heads home to face her new, solitary life.

Maria Samperi has survived one world war and has another yet to come.

Maria Samperi is only twenty-five years old.

'SHE ALWAYS WORE A SHAWL,' my father says. 'Always! And a head scarf.'

'What about in summer?'

'Even in summer,' he says, 'even in summer, she'd wear that shawl.'

Even in the blistering heat of the Sicilian summer, it seemed that my great-grandmother felt a cool breeze.

'Did she ever see the baker again?'

'No,' my father replies, 'at least she never told me that she did.'

'What happened to him?' I ask.

'He died, not that long after that, during World War II. They say he was penniless and homeless. The Americans bombed the town where he was living and they found his body out in the street. He'd been trying to hide under a cart.'

My father picks up the tale of Maria Samperi because he is the one who knew her and her story the best. Of Maria's children, my father's mother and the woman after whom I'm named, was her eldest. My father has few tales to tell about his own mother because as soon as he was able to walk, she packed up her eldest son and sent him across the village to live with Maria Samperi.

'She was all on her own,' my father says, 'and besides, I think secretly, my mother was happy to have one less of us in the house anyway.'

So, just into her fifties, having raised three children on her own and having trimmed almost thirty years' worth of lemons, Maria Samperi took yet another charge into her home. My father. For the next eighteen years, from when he was only little to when he left his island to come to Australia, my father was raised by and lived with his grandmother.

'That is how I know the story of that night,' he says, 'the night she rode up the coast of Sicily in a storm to find her husband. Because she and I would sit around the old *conca* roasting chestnuts and she would tell me the great story of her youth.'

'Didn't she ever remarry? Was there no one else after the baker?' I ask.

'No, she never remarried. Whether there was anyone else who wanted to marry her, or who she wanted to marry, I don't know. She never said—and if there was, I was too young to notice.'

I want to ask where Maria Samperi's life went. By the time the grandson she brought up left for Australia she was an old woman. As she sat on that cart heading home, did she think about how her long life might unfold?

AT THE AGE OF SIXTY-FIVE, Maria Samperi said goodbye to the grandson she had raised as her own son. As a parting gift on the occasion of his great voyage she gave him a gold ring to remember her by. This from the woman whose worldly possessions, after a lifetime of lemons, amounted to her timber bed and the jug and basin she washed her face in every morning.

At the age of eighty, Maria Samperi turned over her wicker stool and retired from the lemon trade. By now, trimming or coring a lemon was to her, the same natural action as breathing. Her quick fingers knew the way all on their own.

At the age of eighty-eight, Maria Samperi buried her eldest child, my father's mother.

At the age of ninety, Maria Samperi buried her second child.

But at the age of ninety-six, Maria Samperi drew her shawl around her shoulders for the very last time. She died of bronchitis, claimed, it seems, by that cool breeze that had been following her all her life. She was survived by her third child, the one she conceived when she found the baker.

I DIG MY FINGERS into the loaf of bread and try the technique that looks so well-practised in my father's hands.

'It seems sad. She spent her whole life taking care of others and was always alone. What did she ever do for herself?'

'I don't know that she had much of a choice. She just did what she had to do because those were the times she lived in. She worked, she cooked, she prayed. She just lived a simple, hard life,' my father says, 'but she wasn't a simple woman. And there was one thing that she did do for herself.'

I free the crumbling hunk of bread from the loaf. I'm going to require some more practice but I know that, for me, in this small gesture and in the smell of lemons, Maria Samperi will live on.

'She went to school,' my father continues. 'When she was sixty-six years old she decided it was time to learn how to write her own name.'

So, after nearly a lifetime of trimming lemons, baking bread and caring for others and just over halfway through her life did Maria Samperi finally do something just for herself.

She learnt to form the letters of her own name with her very own, lemon-scented hands.

Stitching

KERRY GREENWOOD

NO ONE EVER called her Nanna. Too soft, too cuddly a name for Isabel Gilchrist Greenwood, nee McIsaac. She was as thin and delicate as a fencing blade and I was as tall as her when I was twelve, and double her weight. She made me feel like a hulking lump of elephant flesh beside her spun-silver curls and her size three feet. Her wedding dress fitted me before I hit puberty and never thereafter. But she liked me, in her cool accountant's manner.

She had married the love of her life and borne two children without much interest or concern. Her passion, the centre of her attention, was always with Grandpa. Her son, my father, visited her almost every Saturday afternoon, sat in the big leather chair and drank tea with lemon as he never did elsewhere. He took me with him, and after a while he left me there, to learn what Grandma had to teach.

She could sew as cobweb fine as fairy scarves of mist. She could tat, knit, make lace, embroider in all manner of stitches—trapunto, blackwork, gros and petit point—and also construct clothes, though she had no style and her garments were fitting but graceless. She could patch and darn, as no one now patches and darns, topping and tailing sheets, re-sewing seams, re-weaving holes with eyes as bright as her bodkins.

And gradually, as each blood-spotted project whimpered towards a conclusion, I found that I could learn to do it too. Grown stronger, my scarred fingers began to take on the rhythm of the clicking needles. I watched my knitting grow from loosely connected holes to a firm, flat, ribbed length of actual fabric. I saw my sewing improve from ragged 'cat-scratch' stitches, uneven and insecure, to the six or eight even stitches to an inch which Grandma had learned from women whose sewing predated Mr Singer's machines. Eight stitches to an inch for garments. Six stitches to an inch for curtains, tablecloths and napkins. With drawn-threadwork to decorate the edges, ranked and rigid.

Grandma belonged to my world but it was an older world. She was fastidious but every morning she bore out to the lemon tree a filled chamber pot, which she called a 'po'. She washed frequently but only bathed once a week. She doused herself with eau de cologne in hot weather, though she told me that ladies did not sweat.

She preferred to buy a chicken with all its insides, so she could make stock from the giblets, and would stand with both hands plunged into bloody entrails like any Sibyl. Then she would rinse her hands and re-assume her sparkle of diamond rings and then she and I would make small cakes with silver cachoux on them for tea.

I never knew whether she approved of me, but she assumed me like a garment, as though I was a duty, and took me with her when she visited other old ladies, the ferocious moustached sort who disapproved of gels in any form. At such places, banished to the garden, I wandered, eating leaves of fresh mint and trying not to attract attention, hoping to be re-admitted so that I could memorise the rapid, coded conversation, to report later to my mother who mostly knew what the old ladies meant. They spoke of the ills of women, of childbirth and of operations and of pain and loss and infidelity. Very quietly, among the tea and the Nice biscuits and the little sandwiches, they wailed for the sorrows of the female world.

Grandma taught me that gentlemen's ways were strange and the male world was different—and inferior—to the real one, where children were born and lessons learned. She taught me that I should be quiet, sweetly spoken and avoid notice, because a lady never puts herself forward. A lady never uses 'I' in a sentence without thinking first. A lady has control over herself and her temper; and a lady never, ever allows familiarity.

I didn't learn these precepts very well. But Grandma

also taught me that if I kept my desires secret and my plots under my hat, I could do anything I liked with any gentleman, and they would never know how carefully they were ruled. And this was, indeed, a new idea.

And yet, and yet. She drove a small orange Gogomobile when no other women I knew drove cars. She was a professional bookkeeper before she fell in extravagant love with Grandpa at a Michaelis-Hallenstein picnic. He proposed with a box of chocolates. On the lid was a charming lady in an orange satin dress, holding a parrot which was saying 'pretty please'. She kept it all her life. I have it now.

Grandma left her job without a thought and plunged into a lifelong passionate affair. And she found that she was restricted by a husband who had a (then incurable) stomach ulcer. So all her cooking was pale and creamy, no spices, no strong tastes, bland beyond bearing for me, used to my best friend Themmy's Greek food and my own mother's cuisine, strident with savours. Grandma adapted. She was a food reformer, making muesli when the word was unknown in Australia. Her cookbooks are full of notes in her precise calligraphy on how to remove any dangerous elements from a diet of grilled not fried, baked not roasted, baking powder not yeast, milk and cream not stock. No garlic, little onion, no spices, no herbs apart from plain parsley.

Her signature dinner dish was stewed celery. Pale green, fibrous, it tasted of nothing whatsoever and was served with lamb chops. I ate it willingly enough. There was nothing to object to in the dish, but it was like eating lightly cooked face flannel.

Grandma occupied her time like a lady. She learned good German—*hoch Deutsch*—from the Countess Elise, a Blütgrafin, who called once when I was there. The gracious lady rustled in good black silk, scented with freesias, and her embrace dented my cheek in the shape of her diamond brooch. She read me 'Mirror, mirror, on the wall' in German—*spieglein*, *spieglein*, *an der wand*.

Grandma and Grandpa travelled extensively, always in a way which would not impact on his fragile health. They took P&O cruises, from which the menus were casually displayed on the hall table. Grandpa took thousands of pictures of Grandma outside hundreds of sights. She always looked uneasy because she did not like being photographed. And there they are—Grandma looking glumly at a Swiss Alp, Grandma staring sadly at the Eiffel Tower, Grandma sitting disconsolately on the edge of the Trevi Fountain. The happiest picture that I have of my grandparents shows them setting out to go to the Chelsea Flower Show, striding along, arm in arm and smiling. Grandpa grew roses, and Grandma appreciated them and arranged stems of them artistically, whenever Grandpa let her cut some for the house.

Grandma showed me how to set a perfect invalid's tray: a crisp, white cloth with just a modest little motif—a flower or a butterfly—in the corner, cut-glass dishes of jam and marmalade, and a bud vase to make the patient feel better. This was ladies' knowledge, required learning. Grandpa supplied the rose buds.

I found out the uses of sharpened matchsticks in cleaning the engraved bits of the family silver and how to remove onion scent from a knife by thrusting it into the earth.

And then there was Grandma's war work. At the beginning of winter, she wound wool. Shackling me with endless loops of fluffy wool, she'd wind it into balls, each exactly the right length for the project, all the while keeping me amused by reminiscing on her work during the war. She was the generalissimo and trouble-shooter of the Comforts Fund, formed to send nice things to the armed forces. She had in this service unravelled and re-knitted thousands of spavined socks, re-seamed hundreds of wobbly shirts and made two horrible new garments out of each horrible old coat. I can see her hands, deft and tiny, with only a slight shimmer of pale nail polish. No lady wore coloured polish.

And yet the tales of Grandma's youth were scant, and only once did I get a glimpse of her as a girl. At her first dance with her older sister, being given a glass of champagne, and demanding sugar in it because it was so sour.

Grandma kept her own accounts and had her own investments. She and my great-aunt bought the house in which I now live. She attended bridge parties, and won prizes. I doubt she read more than one book a year, not even the wedding present sets of Dickens and Thackeray, because when they came to me after her death the pages were uncut.

She ran fetes and cake raffles for the Footscray Hospital and worked every second week at the Auxiliary, where the volunteer ladies sewed dolls' clothes and layettes for the newborns, mended uniforms and kept the hospital's linen in proper order. Being a volunteer was part of being a proper lady.

And it was there at the Footscray Hospital Auxiliary that I received a revelation about my paternal grandmother. Neat, exacting, aloof, that was Grandma. Skilled and intelligent and devoted, that was her as well. Entirely divorced from the real world of flesh and the devil, or so I thought. But one day at the age of eleven I sat down to a pile of pre-cut, glazed white cotton fabric next to my sewing machine. It was a simple pattern: a gathered frill around the top and the rest of the material sewn into a tube. No armholes. I wondered what these garments were. But I sewed them through one long afternoon, interspersed with cups of tea and cup cakes with pink icing. And finally I asked her, 'What are these things, Grandma?'

'They are shrouds,' she told me. 'Shrouds for babies.'

I thought about this. That explained the design. These white starched tubes were to contain the grief of some mother, a dead child. A once living, heavy, solid piece of flesh, product of nine months' endurance. I thought of my adorable baby sister, with her long-lashed eyes and neat little fingers with perfect nails and almost squealed.

'Well, we can't put them into the ground in their skins, can we?' she asked me. 'And the mothers feel it too much. Shrouds are sewn,' she announced as though it was one of those rules about using silver forks with fish or washing lace in milk, 'by children and old women.'

And I saw the workroom, heaped with sewing materials and redolent of tea and lavender water, as a place where death was present and accepted. Not attended by the scythe-bearing skeletons of my imagination but by those who have always been the layers-out of the dead. The disinfected hospital air ballooned around me, black with nightmares. Abruptly I saw these old Auxiliary ladies as the sharp-beaked plump vultures who followed old battles, the lurkers in morgues, the walkers of graveyards; they were the black witches, hungry for the blood and fat of a newborn child with which to make spells for the bane of all mankind. I smelt carrion; I heard screams.

Then I blinked and looked at them again. They were just ladies. Old ladies. Like Mrs Peters who puffed when she climbed stairs and was always good for a peppermint. Like black-clad Mrs Fratelli who was Italian and still mourned her dead son, lost many years ago; occasionally she boiled over into tears like a leaky kettle. Ladies like Mrs Reynolds whose son went to school with my brother and who had porcelain teeth which clicked. Ladies like my grandmother, who knew what a lady should be—and what a lady should do.

As I recall, I shuddered at the time, with horror and wonder. The nightmarish vision flicked off. I drew a deep breath. I turned back to my machine and went on sewing shrouds. Grandma was right. We could not put the dead babies naked into the ground. No lady would allow that.

The Ninth Life

PADDY O'REILLY

SO HERE WE ARE at Chadstone. The shopping centre that changed our world. Seventy-two specialty shops. A department store. A bowling alley. A fairy castle on the roof of Myer. Here we are at Chadstone, sitting on a bench beside a lawn roped off by tidy white chain in the Garden Plaza. Beside us, the dew on a weedy bush jammed into a container glistens in the morning sun.

I am four years old. She sits beside me, stout and stern, her body encased in a snug woollen skirt with a blouse and cardigan. In the centre of the lawn a glass bowl pipes out music. The radio station 3UZ has landed like a raucous spaceship here in the middle of a neat flat lawn in Chadstone and the DJ, whose mellow voice usually interrupts programming to bring us advertisements for cigarettes and heartburn relief, has emerged from the spaceship to host a junior talent quest.

'Ladies and gentlemen,' the DJ says into the microphone, which grunts and squeals across the scattered crowd. 'Ladies and gentlemen, boys and girls, bald-headed babies, welcome to the Chadstone 3UZ Search for a Star.'

Women stand beside their prams and applaud. Kids jump up and down trying to get the DJ's attention by thrusting up their hands like they're in school. Above us, three large flags snap against their poles in the breeze.

The DJ looks around. He selects children one by one with a curl of his forefinger and they run shrieking towards him. His bristly moustache scrapes against the microphone as he corkscrews a finger at me and says, 'Come on over, little lady.'

I sneak a look. Her face is impassive. She shakes her head. I look down at my feet in their black patent leather mary janes, and I swing them back and forth under the seat. I don't want to watch. The lacy frills on my white ankle socks shimmer as they move.

'Ask Nanna if you can join the quest. Sing a song or do a dance,' the DJ says into the microphone. I know he is talking to me.

Without looking up I can feel she is stiff and still beside me, a prehistoric monolith. My shoes start to clip the underside of the seat. Left then right. I know she hates this. I can't stop. My feet are banging out a message. Don't speak. Left right. Don't speak.

She takes my hand. We stand up and walk away, leaving the junior talent quest entrants chattering and laughing behind us. She is keeping her head high, her back straight. Her navy court shoes tap across the white paving. She will not show she is offended.

SATURDAY MORNINGS she drives me to St Roch's tennis courts in Glen Iris because she has heard they have the best tennis instructor.

'Deeper,' the instructor shouts across the court. The skin on his face is tanned dark and creased like a deflated football because he never wears a hat. 'Hit the ball to the baseline.'

He stands beside a washing basket filled with tennis balls on a trolley and hits the balls to me one after another until the basket is empty. Then I have to run around and collect all the balls and once the basket is full we start again with him pummelling the balls relentlessly across the net at me. This misery goes on for half an hour. I hate tennis. But no matter how often I tell her I don't want to learn tennis, she keeps enrolling me in these lessons.

Summer and winter, skin mottled dull crimson or blue, I run around the court flailing at the balls with my wooden tennis racquet. Whenever I stumble and fall, skidding across the dusty pink surface of the court, *en-tous-cas* gravel embeds itself under the skin on my knees and elbows. If I am in pain I must count to ten. The pain will pass. I am not to complain or draw attention to myself. This is what she learned, this stoic old-fashioned forbearance, and I must learn it too.

Once the lesson is over I walk back to the car where she has been waiting. She doesn't go into the clubhouse and wait with a cup of tea. Rather than put on the face and answer the pleasantly probing questions of the strangers at this club, she waits in the car. She doesn't read. She doesn't listen to the radio. She doesn't watch my lesson. She faces the road and waits, silently, for half an hour in the car. Around her, aloneness gathers like a force-field.

HERE WE ARE AGAIN, the odd couple wandering around the south-eastern suburbs of Melbourne. I've developed a talent for anticipating when someone is about to say the wrong thing. It's the fond look they give. Nanna escorting her grand-daughter around, how sweet. Like now, in the Malvern shoe shop. We're struggling through the annual torture of buying school shoes that pinch and yet seem too large all at once. Half a size too big so I'll grow into them.

The shop lady kneels in front of me. She fits the shoe onto my right foot, presses her thumb against my big toe through the black leather, cups the sole of the shoe and pushes it backwards and forwards on my foot. She opens her mouth and I know I have to speak first.

'I want the other kind, like everyone else wears,' I say loudly.

Shop lady rocks back on her heels and looks at us sitting side by side. Her aqua pants are pulled so tight against her thighs I can see the stitches straining at the seams.

The box containing the left shoe rests on her tweed skirt beside me. As shop lady watches, she lifts the shoe from its tissue nest.

'You don't have to be like everyone else. We'll take these as long as they fit,' she says to me.

Shop lady busies herself with my left foot.

Disaster averted.

NOW WE ARE in the grocery shop. This is the grocery shop near our house. Everyone knows us here. Hello Mrs O'Reilly. Hello Mrs M. This is the way people used to live, before Chadstone. Milk at the milk bar. Fruit at the fruit-erers. Groceries at the grocer. Everyone knows everyone. Some things you say, some things you don't. You never say, Hello Mrs O'Reilly, how's your grand-daughter? Because you know. Despite the white hair, the heavy, exhausted walk, the lined face, mouth drooping at the corners like runny ice-cream. You know that this is Mrs Meta O'Reilly, nee Petersen, mother of little Paddy, shopping at the grocer for familiar food. Everyone knows everything and no one says anything and the level of discomfort is like a broken blister rubbing on each downstep.

There is no comfortable place. If they don't know, they call her grandmother. If they do know, the silence can be equally mortifying.

THERE ARE OTHER CHILDREN, but they are older now. She had those children at a decent age. She was already in her mid thirties, but that was respectable. Twelve years later when her hair was white, when a woman should have long given up sexual intercourse with her husband, she had another child. The head nun of the school her other children attended wrote her a letter and told her 'The Lord has been good to you', as if that would ease the embarrassment.

AT CHADSTONE AGAIN. In the modern world, where no one knows your business. Where you come to shop for clothes and shoes and lipstick to make yourself look younger. It used to be that women got old. Not at Chadstone.

I am ten. How old is Mrs O'Reilly? That is one of those things that must never be spoken about. Perhaps there are families where such behaviour is unbelievable: that some things are simply never mentioned. At my house, if it seems for a second that one of these unmentionable things is about to pass someone's lips, the temperature plummets. The room goes crisp and frosty. Eyebrows and eyelashes start to whiten and skin to crack and mouths are numbed until the moment has passed and the unmentionable has been pushed firmly back into the bowel of the foolish person who attempted to speak.

Today we are at my favourite place of all in Chadstone, Downyflake Donuts. From the street you can watch through the window as a machine squeezes out gobs of dough that plop into hot oil, bob merrily down the bubbling oil causeway, growing fatter and more golden, until they reach a lever that flips them over. Then they float to the end of the oilway and are automatically ejected onto a wire cooling rack. From there, the Downyflake shop assistant in a white and pink uniform with a jaunty cap tosses the doughnuts in cinammon and sugar and serves them up to the chrome counter where we sit on high stools. I am sucking hard because ice-cream has stopped up the straw in my lime spider. Above me on the wall is the Downyflake ditty, which I think is pretty smart, even though I don't understand what it means.

As you ramble on through life, brother,
Whatever be your goal,

Keep your eye upon the donut,
And not upon the hole.

'Hello, Mrs O'Reilly,' I hear from behind us.

It is a shock. We never run into people we know at Chadstone.

'Oh. Hello, Mrs K,' Mrs O'Reilly sitting beside me answers. She's using a 'go away we never run into anyone at Chadstone leave us alone' voice. But Mrs K doesn't seem to know what that voice means.

Mrs K looks harried. She is short and dumpy and her grey hair always escapes from a hastily gathered bun at her neck. Today she has her two older teenagers and her very young child with her.

'I'm just picking up some doughnuts to take home. Bubbie wouldn't stop nagging about it,' she says, indicating the little girl beside her.

'I see,' Mrs O'Reilly says.

Mrs K's doughnuts arrive and she packs them away in her older daughter's shopping bag.

'Well, we'll be off to the bus now. Chadstone's wonderful but it's exhausting, isn't it? I feel like I've walked a hundred miles.'

'There's certainly a lot to see here,' Mrs O'Reilly replies.

'And of course it's harder for us older mothers,' Mrs K says.

I am ten years old. My social antennae are only starting to emerge. They are stumpy and blunt and can't work out very much at all. But right now, in Downyflake Donuts, they are zinging. My head hurts with their zinging and pinging and twanging.

I stare into my murky spider. It is not only that Mrs K mentioned the unmentionable—my mother's age. It is much worse. Everyone knows that Mrs K is not really the mother of the young child holding her hand. Mrs K is Bubbie's grandmother, and her middle daughter is the illegitimate mother. At fifteen, Mrs K's daughter went away then came back with a child Mrs K immediately began introducing to people as her own baby.

Mrs O'Reilly cannot speak. Is she being associated with that deception and all it implies about the life of that family? Better to be mistaken for the child's grandmother when you are its mother.

We are all holding our heads up, but we are drenched in shame. There's so much shame around our neighbourhood you could paint houses with it.

SHE'S TIRED. Each year, more and more tired. Grey faced. She looks younger than her years, thanks to Ponds Cold Cream and never using soap on the face. But not young enough. The white hair and the measured, careful gait and the stoop give her away. People still do it. 'Is that your granddaughter on the court? She's a good player, isn't she?'

My father dies. Before he became ill she typed his business letters, clattering away into the night on a big

Remington typewriter at the dining room table after the meal was cooked and eaten and the washing up finished. Then, when he was too ill to work anymore, she emptied his chamber pot and delivered his meals to the bedroom on a green tray painted with a gay Parisian street scene.

Now she is truly alone. Not just in her manner, not just in her containment. She is on a war widow's pension and in her sixties when the fury of my teen years erupts all over the house.

I wish I knew then what I know about her now. Or maybe, because I was a teenager, it would have meant nothing to me anyway. If you put a blowtorch to shame, a chemical reaction happens. Shame melts down to rage, and when the rage cools it is a hard, glassy substance like a shield, a reflective shield.

She said to me, 'What's wrong with you? How did you turn out like this?'

I said to her, 'This is all your fault.'

I meant, You are too old to be a mother. How old are you anyway?

The calculation method never worked. Start with the age of the house she owned. Subtract the age of my oldest sibling. Add ten years each for dogs I'd seen in family photographs. Divide by the rings on the coffee table. That was as good as any answer I'd ever get from her. She was the mistress of subterfuge. A quick trip to the incinerator at the end of the yard and whoosh, evidence gone. A reek from her clothes of the burned Veterans' Affairs document that might have revealed her date of birth.

I'M TWO WEEKS OFF SEVENTEEN. We don't go to Chadstone anymore. She can't keep up with the way it keeps growing and expanding and reproducing itself like a yeasty fungus. Chadstone is getting younger and younger while Mrs O'Reilly's joints compact and her head sinks into her chest.

In fact, there's no more going out at all. The containment process is now complete. She says she can't see the mothers of my classmates because of the shame I've brought on her. I've been wagging school. Everyone knows. I have a boyfriend. He's awful. He's wrong in every way. Unemployed, wild, angry, roaming the streets all day and night. I chose him particularly because I knew how much she would hate him. She keeps trying to tell me I am ruining my life. She means I am ruining her life.

This day I'm eating a patty cake fresh from the oven. She's at her usual place, sitting on an orange stool with the steps that fold underneath and staring out through the kitchen window, her back hunched like a question mark. This is where we meet now. In the kitchen, in the dining room, in the lounge room, over food. We have moments—as the crumbed sausages split warm and juicy under the knife, as the sticky golden syrup dumplings plop plop in the saucepan, as the butter melts into the tea cake—when it seems like we could almost communicate. Then the moment passes.

She never looks at me anymore. She speaks in another direction. I prefer it that way anyway. Whenever I catch sight of her muddy brown eyes I wonder how she can see out of them. It's as if she's grown a third eyelid.

She shifts her buttocks on the stool, still gazing out through the window, and speaks.

'Have you had intercourse with that boy?'

'Yes,' I answer.

'So you are a slut.'

'If you say so,' I reply, and I walk away, stuffing the rest of the cake in my mouth. When I get outside I vomit the clods of dough onto her lemon verbena.

TEN YEARS LATER. I've come for tea. She's in the steamy kitchen, sitting on her stool. She's sat here so long the feet of the stool have dug craters in the vinyl floor tiles. Even the grey laminex on the kitchen table where she rests her elbows has been worn away to white.

Outside it is dark. On Sundays I visit. Every Sunday I visit and I stay for tea and we chat about the news as we watch a little TV or I do an odd job for her and then I go home. Every Sunday, when I arrive, she asks if I'll be staying to tea. There has always been this formality in her manner, as if I am a stranger who arrived unexpectedly in her womb and she must be polite.

She never telephones me except to say, 'You have mail.'

I arrive home at the share house and my housemate says, 'Your mother left a message on the machine. You have mail.' It becomes a joke. My mother will only speak to me when I have mail. Even when I answer the phone, she says, 'It's your mother. You have mail.' On the phone I cannot engage her in conversation. 'You have mail. All right, dear. Goodbye.'

This night when I am visiting, we move to the table and sit down to eat our honey and mustard pork. The television mutters in the front room. I am startled when she speaks.

'I like it when you come to visit,' she says.

It's like I have watched her open a vein.

THE RECORD of her life has been gutted. Once she chose to hide her age, everything had to go. Letters, birthday gifts and cards, school records, graduation certificates, notices from government departments. It's only after she has died that I find a few things she missed in the purge. I find Miss Meta Petersen.

A witty Christmas note from her employer at 3XY radio in Melbourne, clumsily typed in the form of a memo.

December 1945.
Miss Petersen From 'THE BOSS'
Please note that I want you to observe the following points over the next twelve months? Or do I mean weeks?

> For your patience with me over the past year:
> For your cheery disposition and sense of humour:
> For putting up with Harold Hull, a menace if ever there was one:
> For not cutting Announcers' throats and committing murder:
> For coping with crazy Artists—good taste forbids me to mention names:
> For being just yourself and my favourite Secretary:
> Please accept my very grateful thanks and appreciation for these things and many others—my wishes for Xmas and New Year are deep and sincere and I look forward to being in a position to 'dictate' to you for a long time to come.

Clothes hidden at the back of her wardrobe. A crepe de chine frock. A navy silk jacket with three-quarter length sleeves and big, cloth-covered buttons. A shantung dress in gas blue shot through with gold.

A book my father gave her when they were courting, both in their thirties already, in 1943. Don Marquis' stories of Archy, the cockroach with the soul of a poet, and Mehitabel, his best friend, an alley cat in her ninth life. Archy typed his poetry on Don Marquis' typewriter while Don was asleep but, being a cockroach, he had to hop from key to key to make the letters. As he couldn't be on the shift key at the same time, his poetry had no capitals or punctuation.

Mehitabel's song, as transcribed by Archy
do you think that i would change
my present freedom to range
for a castle or moated grange
wotthehell wotthehell
cage me and i d go frantic
my life is so romantic
capricious and corybantic
and i m toujours gai toujours gai

My father wrote on the flyleaf:

To Dear Meta,
Hoping that I may humbly assist you to remain, like Mehitabel, 'toujours gai, kiddoo, toujours gai!'
With all my love,
Bede

I wish I had met Miss Meta Petersen.

HERE WE ARE at the end. I am thirty-eight years old. She is in a bed in a ward of the repatriation hospital, sleeping, lying on her side, chin to sternum like a folded bird. One day away from death. The chart at the end of her bed. Mrs M K O'Reilly. Yesterday a new tea lady pushed her trolley into the ward and stood behind me, watching me watching my dying mother.

'Is this your grandmother?' she asked kindly.

Today the old woman in the next bed calls me over. She takes my anxious fretting hands in her warm dry ones and rubs them like you would rub the hands of a cold child.

'Don't be afraid,' the woman says to me.

I shake my head and clench my teeth and blink fast.

'She's ready, darling. How old is she?'

I do know. But how could I betray her now?

'I'm not sure,' I say. 'She never told me.'

Extra Lucky

LORRAINE McGEE-SIPPEL

MOST PEOPLE I know consider themselves lucky to have one grandmother. So I must have been extra lucky because although for years I had only one, I ended up with four. They were all very different yet they all enriched my life in their own unique way.

NANNA MASON, my mother's mother, was one of twelve children. She was born in 1878, in Wollongong, NSW and married Fardie, my grandfather, in 1899. Nanna was one of my favourite people, and the first grandmother that I remember. She lived with Fardie and one of their married daughters around the corner from my parents' place in Marrickville where we lived for the first two years of my life. Soon after the Second World War finished in 1945, Mum and Dad threw their factory jobs in. They packed our bags and we headed bush. They had work on country properties lined up.

I didn't get to see much of my grandparents for a while after that because Mum and Dad could only afford for us to come to Sydney once a year on annual holidays. However, in 1949 they both managed to secure jobs back in the big smoke and we returned to live in Sydney for a year. That was the year I started school, at Glebe Public. It was also the year that Fardie died. I don't know if Nanna cried but Mum couldn't stop. Nanna was about seventy then, but I don't remember her being especially old, even though she wore dark hats, a hair net and subdued colours. Maybe her sombre outfits had something to do with her being a 'Sally'. She was in the Salvation Army, and they seemed pretty strict about their dress code and behaviour.

Altogether my grandparents had seven children and about fourteen grandchildren. I was ranked in the middle somewhere. Sometimes I sensed that Nanna had her favourites. Not because she said anything in particular; it was just a feeling I had. Maybe I picked up on it because I looked different to everyone else in the family, and there were others younger and cuter than me.

What I loved most about going to Nanna's was the musty, mothball smell of her house. And I adored the treasures she kept in her bedroom. It was like entering a different world, as if Nan had two lives: the one she presented to the outside world and the one inside her bedroom, which was full of colour. Here all kinds of magical things spilled out of her drawers, her suitcases and wardrobe—the pale variegated silky thread, the half-finished baby clothes, the multi-coloured crocheted woollen squares, stitched together to make a bedcover for someone in the family, generally one of her grandkids. We all got one. Mine was all shades of pinks and blues, with a bit of black and white to make it more interesting.

Mum and Dad also had a crocheted bedspread, but theirs was made of silky white cotton in a delicate lace pattern. It was beautiful and I coveted it for years. My mother had paid Nanna thirty pounds to crochet it for her. It had taken Nanna three years and a lot of love to make this exquisite piece of work for her eldest daughter, and I looked upon it as a family heirloom, one that I might inherit one day. I think Nanna would have been very upset had she known that years later Mum sold it. Why she sold it and to whom I do not know, unless she was short of money. It was hard to make ends meet on rural wages, so Mum tended to book things up, a 'buy now and pay later' arrangement. She had accounts everywhere, some that Dad and I didn't know about until a few years later when my father's wages were garnisheed. She also had headaches that wouldn't go away, and that meant more doctors' bills.

When I asked where Nanna's bedspread was, Mum did her block.

One day when I was eight, I told Nanna in my confident voice that Dad was teaching me to knit. It was easier than crocheting, I said. Nanna pulled my chair close in to hers and gently shook her head.

'No. No, love. Crocheting is much easier. You only need one needle. Here, let me show you.'

Picking her crochet hook up to demonstrate, Nanna proceeded with her instruction.

'This is what we're going to make, this doily for a dressing table.' She pointed to a picture in a pattern book. 'See, it's easy,' she said, patting it like a puppy.

I took the crochet hook from her to give it a go. I had to admit Nanna did make it look easier than knitting, so I don't know where I went wrong. I ended up with a funny-looking cap shape, nothing about it that would ever sit flat. It would have made a good egg warmer. Nanna just smiled and told me not to worry, that it would all come to me one day. And so it did—about thirty or more years later.

One day Nanna gave me a Shirley Temple book. It was big, like an A4 size, what was called quarto, with a sepia picture of Shirley Temple on the cover, taken in the thirties. A Hollywood star at four years of age, a little poppet with curly hair, she was so cute, especially when she sang and danced. I couldn't believe it when Nanna gave it to me, because I didn't even have to ask. Mum always said it was rude to ask for anything, so I never did. But I guess Nanna could see how much that book meant to me because I used to spend hours drooling over the pictures, wishing it were me. Nanna gave me a Bible as well, when I was almost eight, but it didn't have pictures in it so I wasn't all that interested. Later, when I was a bit older I tried reading it, but I couldn't get past all the begatting, so it didn't get read then either. I still have that Bible today, however, fifty-eight years later. I keep it in the lounge-room, on the bookshelf. It sits on top of a nursing dictionary; they seem to go together. The inscription inside says, 'Lorraine from Nanna 1-1-51'.

Nanna had this way of pronouncing my name, as if she were practising musical notes; she would stretch the vowels out, as if they were on a band of elastic, so that my name became two. It was unusual. 'Law Rain,' she would say. That's what Nanna called me all my life. I didn't say anything to her about it because Mum would have clipped me round my ears and told me not to be cheeky. But Nanna never hit me or raised her voice; she was always gentle and kind.

By the time I got to high school I was living with relatives in Seven Hills, having been sent away from home and my parents the month I turned eleven because of not getting along with the new teacher at Isis River School in the country. Nanna had moved too by now and was living in Campsie. Later she moved to another part of Marrickville. I would save my pocket money so that I could visit her. I'd catch the train from Seven Hills railway station to Central, hop off there and catch another train out to Marrickville. It was quite a trek. I never timed it exactly, but when I got back to Seven Hills I'd have been gone about four hours. I'd always take Nanna a bag of chocolate-coated ginger, which I'd buy from Darrell Lea's. She didn't get many treats and these were her favourite.

In 1963, when I was aged twenty, Nanna asked Mum and I to accompany her to Prince Alfred Park, near Central railway station. It was Easter and the Salvation Army had set up a large marquee; it was a special time of the year. I had no idea what I was letting myself in for when I agreed to this. It turned out the Sallies were looking for young people like me. I had been christened into the Salvation Army Church and for a brief period before my parents went bush again had attended Sunday school. It was hoped that I might follow in my grandmother's footsteps. I loved my grandmother and respected the Sallies and the work they did, but there was a limit to what I would do for Nanna. The thought of wearing that hat and uniform, as well as having to collect money and rattle a tambourine wasn't for me, I decided.

When the person walking down the aisle stopped level where Mum, Nanna and I were sitting and looked directly at me, they nodded their head to see if I was interested in committing myself. I was mortified. Pointing to my bandaged knee I shook my head vigorously. No words were exchanged, but Nanna understood. She always did.

Two years after that, in 1965, Nanna died. It was the year she turned eighty-seven, and for me life was never the same again. Mum's youngest sister had phoned to let us know. It was and it wasn't a shock because Nanna had been a bit unwell, though she usually bounced back. But not this time. Mum and I sat together in the black funeral car directly behind Nanna's hearse, all the way to the crematorium at Lidcombe. I wore my black coat and a borrowed hat that day. Mum and I shed a few tears but we knew Nanna would be okay, because she'd led a good life.

BY THE TIME I realised I had a second grandmother I was half-grown. Grandma, my father Allan's mother, was the second wife of Dad's father. They had seven children, and lived in Kurri Kurri, in the Hunter region of NSW. When I got wind of her existence Grandma was already married to her second husband, whose name was Jock and was from Scotland. I didn't know Grandma's name until recently when I did some research and found that Minnie Butts was the middle child of nine, born in 1888 in Quirindi, New South Wales.

I think Grandma and I might have met once but I can't be sure. I do know though that Jock the Scot wasn't very popular with Grandma's family. They called him a miser and said that he was saving his money by starving

Grandma, so that he could go back and live in Scotland. Good riddance, I say. Jock gave his fellow countrymen a bad name, one that they didn't deserve.

But they could well have been right about Grandma being starved, judging by the only photo I ever saw of her. She looked as if she could have done with a good feed. In the photo Grandma is sitting in the sun on a straight-backed chair. Dad is standing on the right of his mother and his brother, Rick, is on the left; Winnie, their sister, is somewhere in between. But the first thing that strikes me is how bony Grandma's face is. Her hair is straight, and the loose plain sleeveless dress hanging off her shows up her bony arms. There's no ornamentation, no beads, no nothing to say that Grandma was cared for, or cared about.

It seems Winnie tried to intervene, along with Dad and their brother, but it was all to no avail. Jock strung them all along until it was too late to do anything for Grandma. She died in 1961 and probably never knew the gift of love she had given me via her eldest son Allan, who was the best father I could have had.

COULD IT BE TRUE? It was September 1981. I'd just got off the phone to my birth mother, Hazel, for the very first time. She'd told me that my grandparents were still alive and looking forward to meeting me, and that she was too.

My grandmother was Aboriginal, she'd just explained, and her parents and grandparents were as well. It was my grandmother who named me Gloria Patricia, I learnt only minutes before. Both she and Hazel had wanted to keep me, but they'd been forced to give me up. It was my grandfather's decision, she insisted, that I'd been put up for adoption. Hazel had spent time in Parramatta Girls' Home, for misbehaving. She was only trying to win her father's love and approval, she said.

Did this mean I was Aboriginal, I wondered. I didn't want to be Aboriginal. Why couldn't I be Maori or Afro-American? I knew more about them than I knew about Aboriginals. How could I be something I wasn't?

I didn't know what I was supposed to say. One minute I was wanted and the next I wasn't. My adoptive father had told me back in 1968 that I was Afro-American, but now my birth mother was saying I was Aboriginal. And she'd told me that she'd been in that hellhole of a place at Parramatta, the very same institution that Flo, my adoptive mother, had threatened me with if I didn't behave. And I'm the eldest of how many grandkids? Fifty! Fancy not finding out you had another pair of grandparents until you were thirty-eight years of age, almost middle-aged.

Later that month I met my mother, Hazel, for the first time. And my youngest brother, Wayne, the following week. Then in October that year, a few weeks afterwards, I met my grandparents, at my cousin Shirley Anne's place in Little Bay near La Perouse. I was so excited that day, not worried about being Aboriginal anymore by now, sure that everything would sort itself out.

I remember Allan and I waiting to be picked up by Hazel and her husband, John. My adoptive mother, Flo, who had died thirteen years previously, didn't want anyone knowing that I was adopted, so I pretended I wasn't, until I couldn't pretend any longer because it was affecting my health. So, I don't think Mum would have approved of this search of mine for my family.

Anyway, soon we were on our way along Anzac Parade. When the car pulled up outside Shirley's small brick home everything seemed to be in slow motion. I'd been told there'd be a lot of people waiting inside to meet me, but just then I couldn't remember a single one of the names that Hazel had rattled off. And I didn't have a clue what to call my grandmother, although it also didn't seem to matter because at last I knew the truth of who I was and for the time being that was all that mattered.

I remember walking up the steps. We're on the landing. We're inside. There's a sea of faces and someone is standing close to me, whispering my name.

'Gloria, darling.'

I know who it is without looking. It's my grandmother. I have waited thirty-eight long years for this day to come. Thirty-eight.

And now I'm turning around and there she is. I see my brown-ness reflecting back at me. Imagine being lied to about something as precious and as important as this. The words are out of my mouth so fast it's as if someone else is speaking.

'Aren't you beautiful?'

I touch my grandmother's shoulder and then her face. She is wearing a powder-blue dress and a white cardigan, the colour blends well with her curly white hair. And those soft brown eyes of hers are brimming with tears behind her glasses.

'You're beautiful too, Gloria darling,' she says softly.

Yes, Gloria. I was Gloria. Not Lorraine at all.

Now my tiny Nan is tucked under my armpits, and we're hugging and kissing through tears of happiness, of sadness, of too many lost years. Overcome with emotions I need to sit down.

And soon I am posing for more and more photos, with Allan my adoptive father, my mother Hazel, with Pop, and with Nan, who is holding my hand in hers for everyone to see.

'Ready? Smile,' says cousin Shirl, the family photographer. 'I'll send you copies as soon as they're developed.'

It was quite a day. And before long I was to discover much more about my family of origin.

Nan was thirty-seven when she became my grandmother, I learnt. And seventy-five when I met her. All up she'd had sixteen children, twelve of whom survived. They were all living in New South Wales. My mother Hazel was the eldest.

My grandmother was Dinah Myrtle McGee, a Yorta Yorta woman, the fourth of eleven children born to Janet and Ernest McGee in 1906 at Moulamein, in south-west NSW. Her childhood was spent on Moonahculla Mission, twenty-five miles from Deniliquin.

One day in 1916, a black car pulled up outside Moonah School. The men, a policeman and his driver, had come for the four sisters who were being cared for by Nan's mother, Janet McGee (nee Ingram), while their mother worked on a station close by. Fear and pandemonium exploded; the kids knew what they had to do. Nan's twelve-year-old brother Osley and his mate Eric got to their mothers fast. The men were all at work on nearby properties. What hope did the girls and their mother have? The youngest of the four girls, Geraldine, was being picked up from Deniliquin Hospital by her great-uncle and aunty, Osley and Ethel Ingram, who were Nan's grandparents. Fortunately she escaped the fate of her sisters. It was heartrending for everyone, but even more so for a mother to see three of her four daughters being dragged away to Cootamundra Girls' Home. The ever-present threat of kids being forcibly removed hung in the air from then on and Moonahculla Mission was no exception to what was happening elsewhere.

Not long after this Nan's large extended family, three generations in all, moved to the outskirts of Barham, away from Mission control. Her father, grandfather and uncles had jobs and were hoping to buy land. Their boss encouraged them. They were good workers, he said. They'd be independent.

And before long their kerosene-tin humpy was built, and they had a vegetable and flower garden. All went well until the land was taken back. Aboriginal people couldn't own land, they were told, by someone or other. The land they had always thought of as theirs was needed to resettle diggers who had recently returned from the First World War.

In 1924, my grandmother Dinah was at a supper dance in Barham with her sister, Lena, and Lena's husband, Bill Harrison, a white man. That night she met the gangly, good-looking Joe Wooding, who was also white and a good mate of Bill's. Introductions followed and a marriage not long after. The following year my mother was born, and in 1927 they left the area and headed to the Riverina, never to return to Nan's Yorta Yorta country or to see her parents and most of her family again.

Did Nan know this when she left, I wonder. Was it then that my grandmother lost her voice? She couldn't—wouldn't—talk about her past to anyone, not even her own children, as much as they tried coaxing. The only family Dinah would discuss the past with were two of her nephews. One of them was Brian McGee, the son of her brother Osley, who had run with his mate to get the mothers before the girls were taken to Coota. The other nephew was my second cousin Jimmy Little, now a renowned singer. Only with these two would Nan share what she had left behind. Was it shame, pain, guilt, or all three that prevented her opening up? I guess I'll never know.

Being the eldest of Nan's fifty grandchildren—we learnt later there was one more—I felt a responsibility to journey back to where she had come from and to connect with her family and descendants, and maybe meet someone Nan had grown up with on Moonahculla. And that someone was Aunty Gerry—the little girl who was collected from Deniliquin Hospital by my great-great-grandparents on that terrible day when Aunty Gerry's three sisters were taken to the home. Aunty was thrilled to see me.

'Stay right there, darling,' she said. 'You look so like your grandmother. We didn't know what happened to her after she left in the sulky that day with her husband and baby daughter. I'm so pleased you came.'

And I was pleased too, and thankful to Aunty Gerry and Nan's mob for filling me in on all the stories. It was like taking Nan's spirit back to her country, and what an honour it was.

Nan was in my life for just a brief six years. And two of those years my husband and I were living on a remote island in Papua New Guinea. However, after twelve months we managed a holiday in Sydney, and were able to borrow a car. We drove to Coonamble to take Nan and Pop out for their sixtieth wedding anniversary.

So really you could say Nan and I shared only four years together. Four quality years, even though we were separated by 600 kilometres; Coonamble is a long way from Sydney. But because of—and maybe despite—the distance, we found ways to see each other as often as we could. I'll never forget the joy of sleeping in the same bed with my grandmother when I went to visit her, and the love I felt as she reached for my hand. I'd wake up with her hands in mine, knowing that these precious memories were ours and ours alone and no one could ever take them away from us.

My dearest Nan, the fourth eldest of eleven, and the last surviving member of her Yorta Yorta family, died in 1987. She was eighty-one.

Having visited my grandmother's country along the Murray and down into Shepparton a number of times between 1989 and 1995, and meeting more and more family each time, the biggest thrill for me was being told how much I looked like my grandmother and her sister, Aunty Ettie. 'She's a McGee. Doesn't she look like Aunty Ettie?' was enough to make me change my name by deed poll, incorporating McGee into my married surname. Hence McGee-Sippel. And that's how I've been signing things ever since 1995.

'I'm so pleased you did that,' said cousin Betty Little. 'Now we know who you are when we see your poetry in the *Koori Mail*. You are one of us, and a strong Yorta Yorta woman.'

I HELD LITTLE HOPE of ever meeting my paternal grandmother. But fifteen years after Nan died, in 2002, I set out to find my biological father, Fred. I had little more than a name to go by, but I was determined I'd find him, wherever he was.

After years of lies, deception and battling red tape, I did find Fred—and his mother, my fourth grandmother. Both were in unmarked graves at Botany Cemetery, near La Perouse. How I wept at the time, as I weep now.

What were you like, Emily Blanche Harper? You died in 1951, when I was only eight. You married a much older man named Walter who died in 1938. You were fifty-six at the time. How did you manage? What were your circumstances? Perhaps the other unmarked graves in this vast, windswept place tell some of the story.

I want you to know, Emily, that although it took years to come about, I met some of your family, a grand-daughter and a grandson, in Leeton. They welcomed me with open arms once they knew I was their Uncle Fred's daughter, the cousin they never knew.

You can be proud of your family, Emily, your descendants. You see, without them I wouldn't have found either you or Fred. And it was you who gave birth to my biological father, who in turn gave me life, and I want to thank you for that. I've already thanked Fred.

The Forgotten

JENNIFER MILLS

SHE IS THE QUEEN of Scrabble. An elderly Welsh woman, her accent makes her seem cartoonishly sweet. She is bedridden by diabetes and a number of other illnesses, but she always has a wide, gappy smile when she plays her favourite board game, and even rubs her hands together. Probably this is because she always wins.

The walls in her corner of the room are completely covered by a collection of postcards. Depicting beaches, islands, cities, castles, they come from places far and near, places that seem almost mythical to me. Exotic spots like Paris or Noosa. I gaze at the walls and lose my concentration on the game; I am small, much younger than her and much more easily distracted.

After she has taken every triple word score on the

board, she asks me to open the top drawer of her dresser. Inside, a dusty block of chocolate and some loose Minties offer a tempered temptation. An offer of compensation for my inevitable defeat.

'Take some Minties,' she says, with her trademark smile.

I take one or two.

'Take a handful,' she insists.

I politely fill my tiny hand.

'Take some for your brothers, now,' she continues.

The pocket of my school uniform bulges. Inevitably, I eat my brothers' Minties on the way home, along with my own. They always have a faint taste of hospital about them.

I like hospitals, though I could do without the various illnesses and injuries that bring me in contact with them. The smell of disinfectant; the weird light; a sense of urgency, as at airports; the morbid fascination of bodies and minds going wrong. It is a strange collection of sensations to be nostalgic for, but memory is nothing if not strange.

MRS A was not my grandmother. My mother returned to work soon after I was born. A registered nurse (RN), she did evening shifts at a local aged care facility. They were still called nursing homes then. As an RN my mother was in charge of some sixty elderly patients. As there wasn't much available in our area in the way of affordable childcare, the nursing home provided my after school supervision. From about the ages of six to twelve, I spent at least one afternoon a week visiting the elderly residents, many of whom suffered from dementia. I had sixty mad, sick, delusional adoptive grandparents.

One afternoon, I wander into Mrs A's room to visit and play Scrabble only to find her asleep. Slack, her face is bereft of its light. Her body is marooned, loose, white and enormous. I feel oddly threatened by the whale-like vastness of her chest, the texture of her seemingly bloodless skin and the precariousness of all this balanced on a wheeled bed. I am embarrassed, but I can't resist staring.

What does it mean to be old? What do the elderly—what does their oldness—mean to the young? There is an instinct to venerate, I think, but it is seriously compromised by a sense of difference. Beneath my nostalgia for the hospital environment, I recall a childhood fear if not of the elderly then of the institution, of the flavour of death and dying. It is generally not until we are adults that we are able to recognise how valuable our elders are as memory keepers, as holders of story. In my white culture this role is rarely valued enough. It is only when memory is lost that we recognise how much we depend upon it for a sense of coherence and continuity—of self, of family, of culture.

The Forgetting, David Shenk's wonderful book about Alzheimer's disease, outlines the process of degeneration in both medical and emotional detail. Broadly, the disease has three stages. The first stage is the most familiar: that of memory loss. The first part of the brain to be attacked by Alzheimer's plaques is the hippocampus—one of the last parts to develop in a child. The hippocampus governs shorter-term memory development. Its loss affects the ability to form new memories. You may forget where you have left your glasses. Soon afterwards, you will start to lose words. As vocabulary drifts away, you will find other ways to communicate.

Mrs R is a wonderfully cheerful woman who always seems to me like a child in an old person's body. She giggles like a kid when she jokes with her small visitor. Her decline is disturbing, but her presence is simply fun. There are other residents who play like children, inventing new words for cups and spoons or pretending to hide from the staff. The first stage of Alzheimer's entails a loss of the inhibitions that prevent many adults from playing. Some residents are a delight to be with, adrift as they are in a sea of memory loss and creative language. One woman only speaks Russian; another old fellow only speaks to the fire hydrant in the corridor. I understand this; I too am prone to conversations with inanimate objects. Other children tell me I am weird. I prefer the company of books and my imagination. In some instances, I prefer the company of my elders.

Alzheimer's disease may strip its victims of their co-ordinates in time, but in a sense they are offered a new kind of presence in exchange. The newfound capacity to dwell in the present moment is much like that of a young child. But this first stage is not all tea and biscuits, Scrabble and Minties. Emotional impulses can get out of control. Outbursts can escalate into violence. There are rooms at the nursing home that my mother warns me against entering: strange, darkened zones inhabited by amorphous monsters who will grab and shriek.

The solidarity I felt with the majority of the nursing home residents was not simply due to our incidental similarities of mind. It was prisoner's solidarity, too. We were all trapped there at the nursing home for a certain term, with my end in sight—when my father got home from work or my brothers from high school—and the old women's end being death. We met each other in a kind of purgatory of supervision. It was never clear who was babysitting who, though I suspect that even at that tender age my sense of my own responsibility was inflated.

Each afternoon I left the nursing home with jaws aching from all the smiling I had to do. Children—even very young childen—often smile at the elderly in the same way adults smile at babies. We are worried that if we stop smiling they will be damaged in some way. Their skin is rice paper, easily torn; their hearts must be as fragile. The elderly are also so unbearably delighted by a young visitor that it is difficult to refuse them any of your charm.

Some days I was resentful of having to go to the nursing home after school when I could have been entertaining my imaginary friends. But usually I took it as given, and appreciated the extra time I spent close to my mother. However busy she may have been managing a ward of sixty people, the ability to loiter on the periphery of her working life made me happy. Besides, I had the luxury of going home every evening, usually with a pocketful of lollies.

> I fear I am not in my perfect mind.
> Methinks I should know you, and know this man;
> Yet I am doubtful for I am mainly ignorant
> What place this is; and all the skill I have
> Remembers not these garments; nor I know not
> Where I did lodge last night.
>
> – William Shakespeare, *King Lear*

THE MIDDLE STAGE of Alzheimer's disease is broadly categorised by a loss of identity. Impulsive behaviour can develop into symptoms which resemble psychosis. Hallucinations, paranoia and aggression are common. Thirty per cent of Alzheimer's sufferers experience illusionary misidentifications or other delusions. Caring for the person becomes difficult as they often deny the disease and resist treatment.

There were people—the grandmothers of other children, some of them—living at the nursing home who believed they were aboard ship, still in Russia, on a train or in a hotel. It was generally acknowledged to be easier on everyone if the staff and visitors played along with these delusions. My mother taught me that any attempt to explain the reality of their situation would have to be repeated every five minutes, and for the patient, that would only repeat the heartbreak and terror of identity loss. At home in imaginary worlds, I wasn't just prepared to suspend my disbelief; I was delighted by the opportunity to do so.

In her youth, Mrs S was an opera singer of some repute. In the evenings, her husband, who lives at home, visits to sit with her in her room. They sing beautiful duets together. Their fine Scottish voices soar down the corridors, and staff and visitors pause to listen reverently. After her husband leaves, Mrs S claws my arm to ask, 'Who was that awful man?'

In a sense, it is not the patient who disappears but their family, thrice denied on every visit. To be forgotten is worse than to forget. The process of feigning can be heartbreaking for family members. Though a loved one is still alive, they no longer share your reality. They have one foot in the other world. I think of Edgar's aside as Lear mistakes a joint-stool for his daughter Goneril: 'My tears begin to take his part so much,/They'll mar my counterfeiting.'

Families can also be our jailers. My memory of the nursing home is coloured with the grey of suburbia, its sense of dull abandonment. I think of stormy Sydney afternoons spent penned in from the rain with other people's grandmothers, a feeling of imprisonment, being captured in time. Was I, that primary school age girl, aware that these women had grandchildren of their own? Did I feel sorry for them? I felt all injustices keenly, but I don't remember wondering about their families. There must have been photographs, stories, gifts, I realise now. Someone must have sent the postcards, bought the blocks of chocolate, found the Scrabble set, kept up the supply of Minties.

IN THE THIRD STAGE of Alzheimer's disease the patient is fully dependent. Language is reduced to simple phrases or even single words before being lost altogether. Emotional signals are possible, but more commonly the brain is so wracked with plaques that the patient exhibits extreme apathy and exhaustion.

In his essay, 'My Father's Brain', Jonathan Franzen observes his father's decline with painfully intimate clarity. He writes of the disease as a loss of autonomy but a retention of will. His father exhibits moments of automatic courtesy that seem heartfelt. Franzen does not believe that his father has 'gone'. He believes, as many believe, that the real person is in there somewhere, struggling to communicate his or her will.

Identity and personality are bound up in memory in ways we can't easily define, but they are not contained by memory. Without memory, without a story, the self doesn't vanish; it morphs into momentary capacities. We see how essential will and impulse are to our humanity.

Quite possibly, the visitor—a family member visiting a loved one for a short time—seeks personality where none remains. It is part of the trauma of the disease that the sufferer's relatives are suffering an excruciatingly slow loss, grieving and yet left grasping at the flimsiest straws of being.

As a child, I did not understand these complexities. I made no attempt to categorise my adoptive grandmothers into abstract capacities. I was simply content, not having known who—or what—was lost, to sit with the person who remained. How could I know? They weren't my grandmothers, who were living elsewhere, in their own homes, and at that stage in their right minds.

These days my maternal grandmother lives in a nursing home, confined to a chair. On the rare visits I manage—we live in different states—she asks me how I like working there. It is heartbreaking, but reassuringly familiar. Other people's grandmothers prepared me for being forgotten. And yet I still experience the need to believe the 'real person' survives. That my grandmother is not a ghost of herself.

In some ways, institutionalised care is inherently sad. For anyone—female or male, of however many years. But particularly, it strikes me, for the aged. Are we so alienated from understanding and appreciating our elders that we abandon them to these places? Are we so overworked, so deep in our debt spiral that we have no time to take care of each other? There is a level of systemic failure, this much is clear, highlighted every time another facility is revealed to be abusing residents or cutting corners.

At the same time there is intense pressure from the corporate sector, which recognises an enormous and growing market for Alzheimer's related products, not all of them pharmaceutical. Psychosocial interventions such as memory games and support groups promise relief for carers and sufferers by distracting the patient. And increasingly, medical interventions are offered which do more harm than good.

Psychotic or paranoid behaviours often provide the most challenges for carers: families and, of course, nursing home staff. Researchers estimate that about a third of nursing home patients in the US have been given antipsychotics. A 2006 study of Alzheimer's patients found no significant improvements over placebos in the majority of patients. A recent *New York Times* article outlined the controversial use of antipsychotics in nursing homes. The article quoted Dr Dillip V. Jeste, a professor of psychiatry and neuroscience at the University of California, San Diego, on the placebo effect:

> These severely demented patients are not responding to the power of suggestion. They're responding to the attention they get when they participate in a clinical

trial. They receive both T.L.C. and good general medical and humane care, which they did not receive until now. That's a sad commentary on the way we treat dementia patients.

As well as pouring money into medical cures, we need to re-examine the value we place on our elders, the pleasure we take in their company. There is a powerful reciprocal obligation between grandmothers and children. Given the clinical evidence for 'TLC', there must have been some health benefit in all that smiling I did. There was certainly a surplus of gratitude on the part of my adopted grandmothers. But for many, access is not facilitated between young and old. At both ends of our life, we find ourselves sequestered away from the adult world.

Just as importantly, we need to value the work of people who are full-time carers in the community. Especially given that the burden of care is only going to get heavier as our population ages and medicine advances. As people are less likely to die the swifter deaths provided by heart attacks and other illnesses, more will die the slow, drawn-out, care-dependent death of Alzheimer's. My parents' generation will become an enormous logistical challenge to mine, and health systems are already projecting the costs.

That challenge will not just be social, but philosophical. We will be forced to re-evaluate not only how we deal with the elderly, but how we understand and value memory per se. With how much flexibility are we prepared to handle the mis-identifications and denials? At what point do your grandmother's stories become lies, outright fictions? When does impulsiveness take the bitter flavour of malice? It is hard not to resent people for behaviour which appears to be manipulative. But to cope with the dissociation of Alzheimer's disease, we will need to learn to attach value to the experience of memory loss. Perhaps children, accustomed to more flexible realities, are best equipped to do this.

THERE IS A FOURTH STAGE to Alzheimer's, of course. None of my adopted grandmothers left the nursing home except via the morgue. (The morgue was in-house, a locked door at the end of a corridor.) Occasionally, though, one of the residents would escape, and for this reason those prone to wander were decorated with a paper note pinned to their back: 'If I am lost, please call this number …' Sometimes one would catch a train and be found many suburbs away, perhaps seeking a long-demolished home or a former workplace. Maybe they were just looking for their real grandchildren, having realised at last that I wasn't one of them. When my grandfather did the same thing in the year before his death, I was prepared to find it funny. I'd already become desensitised.

I was protected from the deaths in the nursing home. By the time Mrs A passed away, I was in high school. I didn't find out immediately, and when I did, I was ashamed. I felt I had abandoned her to my childhood and moved on to the important work of being an adolescent—self-absorbed, wilfully ignorant and trying to hurtle myself into the future. I should have thought to send her a postcard to add to her collection, but our relationship was far too mediated, too bracketed into the few hours a week I spent visiting after school. The product of institutional circumstance.

But memory and identity might be characterised as nothing more than the product of such circumstances. In 2008 I co-curated the art project deLiver, a collaborative postcard exhibition. Another version of Mrs A's postcard wall appears in my novel, *The Diamond Anchor.* The narrator of this story is in her seventies, with a family history of Alzheimer's; she is the first to question the reliability of her memories. When I am working my influences are rarely clear to me, but hindsight reveals that those afternoons at the nursing home left an indelible impression.

Perhaps as a result of my early exposure to dementia, I developed a fascination with neuroscience which, however, I never really pursued. My interests have always been too broad; besides, Oliver Sacks was already writing brilliantly on the subject. More abstractly though, I do owe some gratitude to my unwitting grandmother-babysitters for my ongoing preoccupation with memory and moral responsibility. It surfaces in my need to tell untold working class, queer and feminist histories. I see it in Australia's struggle for reconciliation with our own murderous past. The fallibility of memory, particularly collective memory, lies at the heart of our contested history. The forgotten can cause terrible harm.

However, I don't see my writing as some kind of sandbank against memory loss. Fiction does a different job from history. It opens possibilities to the imagination, creates alternate worlds—delusions, if you like—different from, but reflective of, this one; places where we can safely explore certain psychic terrors or unthinkable desires. Stories invite us to place one foot in that other world, and offer us a safe way home.

The observable experience of dementia also has the potential to take us through the looking glass of memory. Shenk, writing of a potential cure, worries that in losing Alzheimer's disease we may lose its lessons, which can be beautifully instructive even as they horrify us. In many ways, I agree with his assertion that what we call a disease is an integral part of life, a stage as resonant, normal and valuable as childhood. But I am equally horrified by the idea of seeing my own parents succumb to the disease.

I remain grateful for the lessons the nursing home thrust upon me: patience with erratic minds; that there is joy in our obligations to one another, even to strangers. I learned a lot from my adoptive grandmothers. I take a great deal of pleasure in being with my elders, listening to their stories, learning about their lives. I remain enthralled by every kind of mental deviance, fascinated by the relationship between brain and mind, memory and self, will and personality. Truth and story. And while I may be a much better Scrabble player these days, I suspect that for me Minties will always taste of hospital.

The Swing

MARION HALLIGAN

SOMETIMES I WONDER what my earliest memory might be. How far back in time I can go before it becomes someone else's recollection. Memories are notoriously corruptible by the recollections of others, or by photographs. But there are no photographs of this, and nobody else knows about it. The other person involved has been dead for more than forty years. The time is June of the year that I turned three in April, a sunny winter day and I am on my own in the backyard.

My father had built a shed right in the corner, by the sand hills that loomed behind our house and sloped sideways to the sea. We called it the asbestos shed, and I suppose it was, though as far as I can see none of us have suffered from it. In the shed he kept tins of paint, jars of nails, tools; he had a big heavy workbench which was always covered with pots of turps, sheets of sandpaper, old tobacco tins with screws in them, as well as all sorts of junk that might come in handy one day. When we three daughters eventually sold the house we walked away and left the shed just as it was, full of stuff, though we did remove certain things; Rosie, I think, took the wooden ladders which he had built. I have the cobbler's last which sat on the bench, on which he soled and heeled our shoes. Far too expensive to have them professionally done. It stands in my front hall and sometimes I use it to keep the door open. It is rather rusty and has spots of cream paint on it—a lot of things got painted cream in my childhood—and sometimes I think of having it cleaned and powder-coated black but then it would be a cute and kitschy object instead of its proper practical self. I can't remember what Brenda took.

About a metre from the side of the shed Father had put in a solid pole with a cross piece at right angles to the top and from this he hung a swing, a wooden seat fastened by two pieces of rope. Like everything my father made it was almost excessively solid and sturdy; they would never break or fall down, except perhaps under their own weight. On the side of the pole there was a hook, and from this he hung the chickens to bleed, when he had chopped their heads off. He tied their legs together, he would never leave a headless chook to run round the yard, its neck gushing blood; he tied the legs together, chopped its head off with the axe on the block and hung it up until it was ready to be plucked and dressed. I know this, though I did not see it; we were not allowed to watch the chooks being killed.

I loved my swing. So, there is this day, sunny, in June. I am sitting on the swing voluptuously swinging, I am three and several months, I know this because I am being minded by my grandmother because my mother is in hospital giving birth to my first sister who was born in June. My grandmother lived five minutes' walk away, just down the road, in a beautiful old house with a bull-nose verandah, set on a slight rise so that it looked over the whole of the Merewether valley in its round curve back from the sea to the hills. It had belonged to the minister, my mother said, and how shocked Grandma was when she moved in, as a bride I suppose, to find it had rats. Rats! In the minister's house. There was an acre of garden too, though in my time a little less, since a slice had been sold to build a house next door. My grandfather grew vegetables, fruit trees, roses; there was a big Norfolk Island pine with a stone table and benches in its shade, a loquat tree on the side lawn, a back terrace paved with old rose-pink bricks. Auntie Lou who never married, who looked after Grandma into her nineties and inherited the house for her lifetime, was lean and strong and kept the whole thing going; when she died the house was bought by the solicitor handling the estate for an improperly low price. He got rid of the big tree and put in an ugly extension with double garages painted pale turquoise. When I was first married I used to fantasise about living in Newcastle and buying that house. So I was especially angry with this bad behaviour.

The part of Merewether where my parents lived was sandy and scoured by the sea winds; but where my grandparents lived, so close down the road, the soil was rich and that little rise it stood on extended behind it and protected it from the southerlies. My grandfather was a lean and handsome man, very like Henry Lawson without the alcohol, with a gentle melancholy air and a thick moustache. I am fascinated to think of the comfortable, fine house and the good life in it—my mother recalled big boxes arriving from Anthony Horderns and wonderful things being unpacked, some brass candlesticks, which I now have, a mantel clock with etched glass, which I don't, a doll for her—and my elegant grandparents bringing up their six children in it, when I know that his job was as a carter for Arnott's biscuits, driving a large flat-topped dray with draught horses, and later when he lost that job he worked as a sort of porter for a menswear shop in Hunter Street in the city, opening the door for the ladies who came to buy their husbands' clothes.

They spoke well, their manners were excellent, their lives gracious. They had polished wood furniture, they ate off linen table cloths, with pretty china (I wish I had a piece of it) and solid cutlery, and lots of excellent vegetables. Grandma made her salad dressings with egg, not condensed milk and vinegar. She said 'sorlt', whereas the rest of us said 'solt', for salt. She was famous for her fruitcakes, but then all the women in my family were.

My grandfather had come to Australia as a lad, with his mother and a brother, to join the father, but when they arrived he wasn't there. Never did turn up. There was a story that he was an unfrocked priest and that maybe there were other wives, but whatever the truth, great-grandmother had to set to and make a living for herself and her children, who of course had to find jobs. My grandmother's family had come out quite early in the nineteenth century, she and her mother had both been born here—Grandma in a house on the corner of Bull Street, which was a restaurant called El Toro when I was at university. I don't know what trades they worked in; but my grandmother's forebears had been cotton spinners in Lancashire, and Grandma was apprenticed to a dressmaker, which meant that she worked for nothing for three years and was then considered to be trained. I have a photograph of her in a dark dress with a long bodice and a tiny waist, exquisitely boned, with ruffles, leg-of-mutton sleeves and a high, banded collar with a horizontal brooch. Her small bosom is round and pouting. She sits slightly oblong in a cane chair; I imagine the boning keeps her at an angle. She is holding a book that she isn't reading, and is pensive, looking sideways out of the photograph, unsmiling, pretty, her curly hair smoothed. Even her name is beautiful: Louisa Emily. In her nineties she had the same slender figure and fine bones (her own, not the dress), and all her life she was a clever seamstress. The unmarried daughter was a milliner; she worked in a shop. My mother learned dressmaking at the tech college, but she never worked; she stayed home with Grandma and was a help. I think she did the cooking and cleaning while Grandma sat over fine handiwork. No wonder when my father proposed to my mother a second time when she was thirty-two she said yes. The women of my family were all beautiful needleworkers; I thought I would be too but it never came to anything; but, I do like to celebrate their skills in my words.

In her seventies my great-grandmother decided to marry again. Her son didn't approve. He forbad his daughter, the milliner, to make her grandmother a bonnet for the wedding. Maybe he was wise; the marriage lasted only three weeks and shortly after the old lady caught a chill and died. Great-Grandma seems to have been a bit of a terror. My mother remembers going to visit her as a small child; Great-Grandma would hoik up her skirts to find a penny for my mother in the pocket in her petticoats. She also offered her small nips of port, saying, 'Won't make you tight, won't make you tight.' Grandfather's house was strictly teetotal; he'd have had a fit.

Anyway, back to the swing. It is a winter day, naturally, being June, quite cold, but sunny. I am warmly dressed, possibly in a fir-green pleated skirt and a jumper of the same green and dark red and beige, which my mother knitted. I hated it because it wasn't pastel and pretty, but looking back I realise it was very smart and just the sort of thing I would dress my daughter in, but I don't remember that this is what I was wearing. What I do remember is that I had tied around my head a piece of gauzy cloth, oblong, pale almond green, embroidered in the corners, what was called a throw-over. When you set your tea table, or supper table, with its little sandwiches and scones and slices and cake, you threw this light cloth—it was not heavy and linen, but muslin, so as not to disturb the food—over the table to keep the flies off. So I have this throw-over tied around my chin, my mother lets me do this. I think she was a very kind and loving mother, looking back on it, she didn't refuse me much, though once when I said to some neighbourhood children that she might take us to the beach that afternoon and they turned up all nicely dressed and ready, first my mother knew about it. I was standing in the laundry tub having my feet washed and she rubbed my mouth with soap for telling lies, which I did not think I had done exactly, she wasn't a wimp at all, and sent the children home very firmly, going to the beach that afternoon wasn't at all on her agenda. But playing with the muslin throw-over was perfectly all right; she probably wasn't into afternoon teas at that time.

Anyway, it was June, and I was dressed warmly. The swing moved quite gently, I didn't like violent swinging, I was singing to myself, I was a bride with a wedding veil over her head, remember, for a little isolated girl brides were even better than princesses, because you know they exist, there is a chance that you will be one some day. I was a bride drifting backwards and forwards in that state of mindless bliss that you don't get much chance of in a rackety world. And of course it was interrupted. Readers know that already, though I have spun the moment out since my first sentences, they have been waiting for something to go wrong, states of mindless bliss cannot last. My grandmother came storming up the backyard in a state of great fury. She was beside-herself-angry with me.

I have thought about this from time to time. I didn't know then and I don't now what upset her. She seemed to be angry that I had taken the muslin and put it round my head. I tried to say that my mother let me, but she couldn't listen. She yanked me off the swing and hauled me indoors. I would have been crying. I can still feel my bewilderment, my misery. I liked to be good, especially outside the immediate family. I say to myself now, well, I suppose she was tired, keeping house, looking after a small child, having dinner ready for my father when he came home from work then walking back to her own house and her own dinner, perhaps it was all a bit much for her. She was, I suppose, quite an old lady by then. She'd been born around 1870 so she would have been in her seventies and had already brought up six children. She'd been used to my mother doing the housework for her but my mother had been married for more than six years by now so she must have got over losing that. All her children, except the milliner, were long married; her eldest grandchildren were themselves about to start. But however I think about it, hers still seems a strange reaction to a small child making her own pleasure. Did Grandma think I was up to something wicked? It didn't seem to occur to her that I would be missing my lovely gentle mother, that the household was in a certain turmoil, and now I come to think of it that my father was preoccupied too, that he would have had to catch the bus and walk up the hill to the old Merewether mansion that had spent some years as a home for unmarried mothers—fallen women—and was now a maternity hospital, and that he would have to walk home afterwards; no, he would have come home from work, had his tea and then walked up to the hospital, so I suppose Grandma had to stay and she was having a long day too and that must have made her grumpy.

I don't remember her ever being cross with me again. Later I stayed with her, maybe that was when my second sister was born, and I remember being quite sick with homesickness but not because of anything anybody did. And then when I was sixteen and had finished the Leaving Certificate my father got me a job at the State Dockyard; the family went on holiday to Nelson Bay for a fortnight and there was no question of my staying home by myself. I enjoyed staying with Grandma and Auntie Lou. I asked my friend Pat to come for afternoon tea and we sat at the stone table under the pine tree; it was wonderfully cool and shady, unlike the yard at my house which was grass and garden beds and hot sun in the December heat. It was around this time that I went to a nursery and got advice on trees that would grow by the sea: pohutekawa and Norfolk Island hibiscus. I gave them to my parents for Christmas. They flourished, and twenty years later when we were selling the house we put the family dining table out under them and ate all our meals there, in a last Christmas feast. But that afternoon when Pat and I sat and gossiped under Grandma's tree it was an unusual thing to do, it was not yet the time of the mandatory backyard garden setting.

So that is my memory of my grandmother, and it is my earliest memory, and it is a mystery. I don't know why my usually mild grandmother was so angry with me that day. I don't remember anything else of that time, not my sister coming home, not seeing my mother after probably a fortnight's absence, not having a baby in the house, and I suppose I should be grateful to that anger; it made a memory.

In the Name of Asher Tiger Jakob John Cox

EVA COX

I HAVE RECENTLY and belatedly become a grandparent, so I am describing what is still very much happening. It wasn't something I had always expected, nor could I draw on grandparenting memories from my growing up. My early childhood was as a wartime refugee in England, which occasionally produced two mysterious old relatives: a great-aunt with two sons and a bachelor great-uncle who lived in a very small flat on his own. Neither seemed interested in, or was interesting to, a small girl. A stray uncle appeared once or twice in army uniform, but breached my trust by failing to deliver some chocolates, so relatives were not big in my early days.

When I arrived in Sydney, aged ten, I acquired a real grandfather (Opi), who was significant in a fairly male way. His second wife, whom we all called Stella, was not a real 'family' member. There were a few more great-aunts and uncles but I have no memories of a close relationship with any grandmotherly figure, actual or surrogate. So the following reflections are really an exploration of something quite new in my experiences.

A grandchild wasn't on the horizon for a long time. My daughter was close to forty before she raised the possibility. Then there was the process of IVF, and I knew the success rate was not high. Even when the first cycle worked, the pregnancy seemed somewhat unreal: would it finally produce a baby? I was supportive but didn't want to invest emotional energy because I was scared something would go wrong, but it didn't! So a grandson arrived in April 2006. Asher Tiger Jakob John Cox has in the last couple of years wound his way into my life and added many pleasures, a new set of future anxieties, and a big new dimension to my sense of the world and its offerings.

The relationship between us wasn't a sudden lightning bolt of emotion, but more of a slow getting to know/finding of each other. My first tentative moves were also about sorting out a new set of expectations, so getting to know the baby bundle became an ever-increasingly joyous mutual discovery. As Asher became more aware of me and I connected to him, we grew links that blurred the edges of our selves, knitting us together in an intense relationship of many dimensions.

Now somewhat over two, he is intensely a person with daily increases in language skills that allow him his own ways of defining the world. On the day I started writing this, he arrived with his parents, banged his small fist on the rattly glass of my front door to signal his arrival.

'Nanna open it,' he was calling.

And when I did, he found this hilarious. This was to be a brief stop as we had planned to go rapidly out to a Sunday yum cha but Asher had a different view. We were confronted with a small bundle of dissent, a toddler's definitive 'no' to the suggestion of a trip on the light rail, and then a big 'yes' to a suggestion that his parents should go and he'd stay with me. He pushed his parents towards the front door, waving goodbye, and turned around to assert his new control as he set the scene for his pleasures.

Asher has a series of routines that symbolise his control over me and my home, so first he moves us from the front door. 'Sit Nanna' commands my presence next to him on the couch as he produces a book he has brought to share with me. A game of pretending to eat multicoloured tinsel stars follows and we exchange views on whether blue ones have different flavours to red ones. He giggles and I enjoy his pleasure in both being in the present and imagining a fantasy. He decides to move to the sunroom and demands to be lifted into his high chair, which he clearly sees as another symbol of his place in my house. (On an earlier visit, he arrived to find the chair was in the dining room and he crossly demanded it be put back at the other table where he thought it belonged.) Then he climbs down, pleased to show his agility, and moves on to opening the kitchen cupboard door to take out his favourite six willow pattern blue bowls so he can line these up on the floor.

He counts, waving his finger towards them.

'Five,' he declares triumphantly.

'No, six,' I argue.

But he ignores me, and the evidence. After all, numbers are still only symbols to recognise without a necessary logical connection.

He decides to show me how he can jump over the plates. The two-year-old feet in small trainers just clear the edges as I watch him anxiously, wondering whether he will slip and/or break the bowls. I open another drawer and offer two plastic containers as an alternative hurdle and he cooperatively agrees to try these, but soon has had enough of that option. He moves to another ritual he previously has established. He goes over to the pantry and demands 'Nanna, sit here', meaning on the library stool I use to get things off high shelves. He joins me to perch on the cat-litter bag for a brief ritualised moment before moving on to something else. I wonder why it is so important to him that we follow the same routine each time he comes to my place.

And so we move on and both enjoy the unplanned two-hour being-together stretch of small boy exploration of place, space, language and relationships. Big giggles occur as we try to both share the chaise longue on the back verandah, which offers a view of the light rail emerging from the tunnel at the bottom of the hill. We sit side by side, then move back to back and I try lying gently on him, as if trying to squash or move him from the same space. He pushes me up and then pulls me down so I almost lie on top of him again and need to hold my weight on my elbows. His apparent ability to have control over my body movements delights him, even though I carefully prop myself up and down. Up and down I go at his command until I have had enough for my taste, so I swing him over me to give him a big hug and cuddle and offer him some food to distract him into something else.

'Want some lunch?'

Yes, to pasta with butter and no to anything that looks as though it might be good for him, like fruit.

I suppose all doting grandparents think their grandchildren are special but Asher suits me! He has a distinct sense of humour and love of language, and as I listen to how he strings words together, I savour the delights of his new sentences. 'Can I help you?' comes out, often followed by 'There you go!' Sometimes 'Wait a minute' emerges from this small boy in strangely adult tones, suggesting a mimicry that intrigues and involves me in his ways of seeing and doing.

SO WHY WRITE such a detailed description of some probably very ordinary interactions between a small boy and his grandmother? I want to explore and share my experiences of this relatively new relationship which is so acutely and surprisingly pleasurable and, for me, extra-ordinary. I watch this small person in ways I have not watched a child before, as observer and participant in a process of growing a child in a very new time. The pleasure in this role seems to me very different to my remembered pleasures in mothering my daughter.

It's hard for me to define the difference between being a mother and a grandmother, and maybe it is partly explained by the unexpected arrival of this small person. Maybe the relationship is different because he isn't so much a total responsibility, the way one's own child is. The closeness is shared with his parents, so we are jointly still very much part of the magic inner circle of family. But what I find interesting is how much he is also clearly separate from us all, a person in his own right.

I am Asher's only functioning grandparent, so this may also make me feel this child is uniquely related to me. His existence connects me to thinking more personally about the future in a time when this is not necessarily a comfortable consideration. We are now surrounded by many, many dire predictions and doomsayers. Of course future gloom isn't new. I remember the sixties, when my daughter was born, had its own harbingers, like the Club of Rome. But in those days gloomsayers who predicted dire limits to growth in the then near future, didn't seem to be quite as scary. The mid-century times were generally more optimistic about the future, and so it made it easier for us to dismiss the predictions as unlikely.

These are more pessimistic times and now climate change seems to have started and other horrors seem more plausible because we have lost faith in presumed progress, which over the last decades has been very costly and not always positive. I realise I will need to engage more of my attention on environmental issues because I now have a more direct connection; I have worked out that Asher will be fourteen in 2020 and only forty-four in 2050.

Because I am still active politically in many areas, I feel a need to extend my issues of concern to those that may affect what could happen to my grandson. This personalised involvement was not so clearly evident when I didn't feel an emotional personal connection to future possibilities. Writing this makes me stop and think what this perception means. I feel somewhat uneasy about the ethics of being involved in worrying about a particular future because of this personal connection. Do the bloodlines make a difference? Shades of the selfish gene! I hope not because I've never been particularly attached to the arguments that we protect our own differently. It seems somewhat callous and rather too Darwinian.

Maybe it is just because I feel the connection with this child, which is closer than that I have to any other from that coming generation, and have some responsibility for him. I think I would attach the same meaningful connection to other children within similar or even wider sets of relationship potentials because of my recognition of continuing relatedness and because there are ongoing commitments.

The last paragraph has made me stop and think about what I said. I realise that the new connection hasn't reduced my wider interests. Rather, the reverse is happening: I am now much more aware of other small children. In my daily trips to the local coffee shop, I instantly notice small voices and bodies and am acutely aware of their presence in the street and elsewhere. I anxiously watch these small persons as we pass each other or share the shop spaces, and worry if they are moving too far away from their carer and maybe putting themselves at risk. I am relieved when their adult notices the risks they take and resumes control. I have stopped the odd runaway and exchanged many friendly empathetic grins with those in charge of small people. This awareness is definitely new, and I respond very much to children of Asher's age and younger. So his existence has resulted in my wider daily awareness of other children, and gives my political self an extended passion to make the world a safer place for them all.

This experience makes me reflect on how my role as a mother in the mid sixties deeply influenced my political activities over the next decades. I was a single parent so my battles to find a childcare place and the then opprobrium of being a working mother pushed my feminist involvement into taking on childcare policy in 1972 when I joined the Women's Electoral Lobby. I was able to influence some policy changes in this area over time in early childhood services, and I also started the first federally funded after-school care service in Paddington, so my daughter had somewhere to go.

In the post-war period, most of us just had children, and had them fairly young. The 'baby boom' made it almost mandatory to populate and not worry; we would manage somehow. Contraception was dicey, though when the pill arrived around the sixties, we gained better control over our fertility. But childcare was not publicly funded, women earned less than men doing the same work and could be denied jobs just because they were female. The experience of mothering a girl fed into my long-term interests in feminism.

Times have changed, and having and rearing children is no longer the rather casual commitment we made. Now it seems very different and parents take it much more seriously. There is wide anxiety to do the right thing and new parents go well beyond an occasional foray into Dr Spock for advice. Having babies later, intensified workplaces and much extra focus on making sure parents are finding the right way to do things, all seem to be part of that platitudinous term, the Zeitgeist, the temper of the times that defines so much of what is acceptable.

So grandmothering is caught up in the complexities of anxious child rearing. And I do worry. Asher has types of allergies I can't remember from the sixties, and bad behaviours are seen as signs of great portent. Is an occasional biting foray a sign of some innate disturbance or just a passing protest against something that can't yet be expressed in words or other ways? Should he be encouraged to take risks on high slippery slides or avoid the possibilities of damage?

This touches on another broadening of my experiences: the gender factor. Asher is more or less my first ongoing close relationship with a small boy. My child rearing was female: my daughter and inevitably her friends, and the mainly female children of my friends. I wasn't a great success at non-sexist child rearing though I tried offering Lego and jeans. My daughter has written about the trials of having a mother who wanted to bring up a child without pre-programmed feminine traits but failed because she actually wanted Barbies and skirts. Now I spend time with a little boy with a clear interest in trains, cars and boy stuff. Dora the Explorer doesn't rank as well as the male Wiggles or even Captain Feathersword, in Asher's view of the world!

And trying to shop for non-stereotyping playthings seems much harder now as almost everything in the toy/child areas is character branded and clearly marketed to attract either boys or girls. There are shelves of girl and boy toys, and aisles of pink, pastel clothes and ones more drearily darker for boys, leaving a still actively feminist grandmother in a shopping dilemma.

I wonder whether being a grandmother will energise me on further political issues, maybe this time more connected to boys? As I have indicated, my personal experiences have been the source of much of my political involvement and I wonder now where else my grandparenting experiences will take me. I am still involved in what were defined as women's issues, matters that we have failed to deal with, such as maternity leave, but maybe I need to be more vocal about parental leave and other forms of workplace re-organisation that makes childcare/paid work integration more normal and less fraught for men and women.

Asher goes to childcare, which is an area which still engages me politically because it is still problematic, and his situation reinforces my involvement. Childcare is still sparsely available in the inner city, so Asher has had too few choices, and that worries me, as I add my perceptions of what I see at his centre to my wider understanding. I listen to my daughter and the others in the mothers' group trying to work their life balances and realise how little has been changed in workplace cultures. There are also questions of fees, staffing and qualifications that are very much on the current political agenda.

I always strongly supported increasing the ratios of adult carers to children for under-twos but now have seen it in action. Last year, I would have been deeply concerned had Asher's centre stuck with a ratio of 1:5, as that ratio seemed to be seriously deficient. Caring for two-year-olds at 1:8 still seems to me to be absurdly limited. I wonder at times if my grandson's sometimes noisy demands for attention from adults at home may be his response to a big centre and too many kids in each of the care groups.

Where are the supportive care services that we saw as extensions of the home and community that would build networks for families through the centres? While there was always a mix of community and commercial services, now there are mainly commercial ones and many of these are run purely as corporate businesses not community services. While the differences between centres don't necessarily reflect the auspice, the current funding encourages economies of scale and undermines the localisation of services. Paying parents, not centres, means that governments have lost their point of influence and services for children can become just another service, like laundromats. The pay rates are too low as care for children is undervalued, seen as a feminine attribute rather than a workplace skill.

So Asher's experiences reinforce my involvement, further reinforced when I met his childcare centre owner recently at a government consultation. The connections became political and personal. However, being an acknowledged national expert in childcare policy fails to give me much street cred in any family discussions on the matter. I become conscious of all of the stories about interfering and overly demanding grandparents, and realise that I should butt out. So I have learned to be less prescriptive privately than I am publicly in making suggestions for changes.

I remember resenting my mother's judgements of my own child rearing practices but used to attribute our tensions to deficiencies in our relationship and her disapproval of me and my political involvements. Now I sometimes sin by saying how I feel and create in Asher's parents some similar sense of feeling judged. So the pleasures of new relationships need also to sit alongside the recognition that some intergenerational tensions may continue, even without political differences.

This is all part of the juggling that comes from sorting out relationships when another generation appears. When our parents die and we lose our status as children, it subtly changes the way we feel about ourselves. When our children then have children the lines extend downwards as they become parents and clearly adults in their own right. This requires shifts and explorations that are very new.

In our family I was an only child, my daughter is one as well. We have half siblings and step siblings at both levels, but there is a clear line of one of us per generation. So neither of us had the models of other siblings to learn from. Asher has to deal with the adults exploring what parenting and grandparenting mean; he has to train us too.

What is the world going to be like for Asher and his generation in the future? We started a revolution in the seventies, or rather picked up on one that had stalled. What we wanted was a world that did not allocate power, privilege and resources on the basis of gender. I grew up being told that I couldn't do/have/expect certain things because I was a girl, and I resented that from a very early age. I am sure no kindergarten would these days refuse a girl a drum and offer a triangle instead as being more suitable, but there are still barriers that gender children in their growing up and adult options. We still have clear and strong divides between the paid workforce and the rest of our lives, with workplaces still reflecting male cultures about time spent there and what is seen as valuable. We still have boys being expected to be masculine, strong and providers. There are still problems for boys who fail tests of being macho yobbos, and too many girls who see this type of behaviour as admirable and to be copied. I am not arguing for androgyny or denying there are gender differences, but I am arguing these need to be equally valued and available as choices for all.

I don't want Asher to have to make limited choices, so this reinforces my sense that it is time to focus on cultural changes, not just the structural ones we have achieved. While boys have had more choices in the past than girls and men still hold most of the powerful positions, they have fewer options to assume those roles that are deemed to be 'female'. As an example, we need to pay childcare workers more so the job is also attractive as a career for men. Taking time out to care for children, or others, needs to be a paid-for leave option that is equally attractive to both men and women. In a future that will involve major environmental, social and technological changes, we cannot afford to stratify choices along gender lines, because we will all need to adapt to very different challenges.

I am a political person, and politics is something that deeply engages me, because I want to fix the world. This probably comes from my experiences as a refugee child. Recently I discovered this fits with the Jewish concept of Tikkun Olan ('mending the world'), so I make no apology for my blending of the personal and political. In writing this somewhat rambling account of my feelings and thinking, I have explored some ideas I hadn't articulated before. I spend much of my time doing what needs to be done because I can, but this activity is now interspersed with the immediate pleasures of my grandson's company!

So far Asher is another only child, but hopefully with a sibling to come. But being just one at this stage makes him particularly precious to me. I've not had the experiences of some friends who had multiple children who have produced multiple grandchildren, so make my conclusions based on a singular relationship. This reflects the richness of my experiences with my grandson that come from the familiar 'one adult and one child' relationship that is uniquely ours.

My Many Grandmothers

SHALINI AKHIL

IT WOULD BE EASIER to write this if I wasn't Indian. As I see it, if I had a non-Indian background, I'd have only two stories to pick from—one about my maternal grandmother, and one about my paternal grandmother. Or groups of stories, even—I'm sure the kids from *The Brady Bunch* had two sets of each. But my family situation is not so simple. In my life so far, I have known many women as many different versions of grandmother—so many, in fact, that when I set out to write this I had to sit down and draw up a list. I've managed to whittle the list of my many grandmothers down to four. But before I dive into their stories, let me give you a glossary of sorts, as I attempt to explain something about how Indian family relationships work.

There are two words for grandmother in Hindi, or at least the Hindi that I grew up speaking—Fiji-Hindi, a pidgin-ish version of the language that came across from India on a ship called the *Leonidas* at the time of the British Raj, when my forefathers came to Fiji as indentured labourers. *Naani* means maternal grandmother, and *Aaji* is what you call your paternal grandmother. They are wives to your grandfathers—respectively, your *Naana* and your *Aaja*. All pretty uncomplicated so far, and that's where it should end for most people as far as grandparents go, but for me this is where things start getting tricky.

Let's employ a bit of creative visualisation to put this into perspective. Imagine Naana and Naani, Aaja and Aaji all sitting comfortably beside each other somewhere near the top of your family tree, a diagram a bit like the ones you drew in biology class when you were learning about genetics. Now, take your pencil and draw a horizontal line below these grandparents; close your eyes and imagine that line extending from left to right till it goes right around the universe and loops back around to join up with itself again. Now, left-click the paint bucket tool inside your head, select a colour and shade in everything above that line. Anyone, anywhere, who falls inside this shaded area and is even vaguely related to you or your extended family—and I use the term 'related' very, very loosely, you understand—is also either an Aaja or an Aaji, a Naana or a Naani, depending which side of the tree they fall on.

MY MATERNAL GRANDMOTHER, my Naani, has ten children, of which my mother is the eldest. Though Naani is generally based with one of her younger daughters in Wellington, she visits her other children in Auckland, Canberra, Fiji and Melbourne, where we are. My parents, aunts and uncles pool their financial resources to buy her tickets to and from their homes.

Earlier this year, she had come to stay with my mother for what was initially going to be a few months, but in the end it turned out to be just one. Naani had stayed with us before, many times, back when we used to live in Fiji. My memories of her stays with us are mainly good; they were generally happy, boisterous times, full of food and family gatherings. She was always around in the days when we spent weekends and holidays with my mum's side of the family too. But the tone of Naani's stays with her adult children has changed recently.

When I was younger and we lived in a large farmhouse in Drasa, a village about twelve minutes by car north-west of Lautoka, my Naani would come to stay with us. I used to look forward to these times with nervous anticipation, because they always involved some sort of upheaval—mostly in the form of a tussle for power between my Naani and my parents. Naani would begin her subtle shifts in the daytime when no one else was around to challenge her. Sometimes we would leave for school and work and come home to a pantry that had been totally re-arranged, my mother's kitchen filing system completely replaced by a new, 'more organised' way, one that carried Naani's stamp of approval.

My brother and I found amusement in my mother's frustration at being ousted from the seat of power in her own household and her demotion back to the status of daughter again. We would encourage Naani as she pestered my mother to have a shower as soon as she stepped into the house after a day at the office; Naani insisted that having a shower too late at night wasn't good for the constitution. My brother and I would wickedly collude, expressing mock concern to our grandmother about our mother's wellbeing until, harassed and tired, she would go and have a shower just to get Naani off her back.

During her stays, my father and my Naani would start out fine, teasing and joking with each other till the novelty wore off. My mother would eventually become the meat in the sandwich—she'd find herself with my father in one ear, Naani in the other. The inevitable explosion would see Naani retreating to her room in a huff to play solitaire (ironically, a game that we knew as 'patience'). The slap-slap as she shuffled her cards would be audible from the lounge room where my father sat most evenings with his eyes closed, clutching a glass of scotch.

I remember once when I was younger writing a poem for Naani's birthday. It was short and it rhymed, and it was full of grandmother clichés I found in books I read at the time: baking apple pies, telling stories on sleepovers. I never baked a pie of any description with my Naani, but she did tell me many stories. About the war, about her husband, my Naana, who had passed away when I was a baby, about the years she spent teaching children, about my mother and her siblings. She told me about her mother, and how her hair had remained jet-black till the day she died. The stories she tells these days seem to wander in and out of memory and imagination. I recognise faint glimmers of reality in them, disconnected events re-arranged and re-told. These days, Naani also pesters me to have children—she points at my husband, then me, pats her own belly, saying '*baby banao*'—literally, 'make a baby'. She reassures me that while I am not the heaviest of all her grandchildren, I could still stand to shed some pounds.

My brother goes along with my Naani's foggy memory; he answers the same questions from her with patience and good humour each time they are repeated. But they stress my mother out, as if she is refusing to acknowledge that Naani's wandering mind could possibly have more to do with her advanced years than her stubborn nature. My mother, suffering the after-effects of a serious illness herself, is no longer able to endure challenges as she once did, and she finds herself physically and mentally drained by my Naani. This distresses her; I talk to my mother, directly and indirectly reassuring her that she is a good daughter. Our relationship changes shape and colour with every passing year; I wonder what it will be like when I am fifty.

WHEN I WAS about nine years old, my family spent a few years living in my grandfather's 'family compound' in Lautoka, the second largest city of Fiji, situated on the western side of the main island of Viti Levu. My grandfather owned four adjacent blocks of land at the end of Malolo Street, which was not far from the centre of town. Two of the blocks—the corner one and the third—were empty, and on the second and fourth blocks stood double- and triple-storey blocks of flats. We lived in one of the ground-floor flats of the double-storey block. Aaja and Aaji lived on the top floor of the triple. On the first floor of the same block lived two more Aajis—my Aaja's sister, Fua Aaji, and my Aaja's mother, Ram Ram Aajia. Fua Aaji scared me a little, as she had a short fuse and a huge overbite, but I think it's safe to say Ram Ram Aajia was my favourite grandmother figure.

Everyone called her Ram Ram Aajia, so it was a term that we in the family were well used to. But it put a smile on the face of anyone hearing it for the first time. 'Ram Ram' is a Hindu greeting—the equivalent of saying 'May the lord Rama be with you'. Everyone greeted Aajia with a cheery 'Ram Ram!' before bending to touch her feet, a sign of respect, asking for her blessing. And she in turn would joyously bestow blessings on everyone, repeatedly patting their heads as they bent before her, a ready grin lighting up her face.

When I first met Ram Ram Aajia I was fascinated by her. She came to Sydney for my father's graduation when I was around seven years old, and I fell in love with her immediately. She always wore white cotton saris with broderie anglaise edging, and she was only a little taller than I was. She had wispy snow-white hair that she always tied in a bun, and the pallu of her sari always covered the top of her head. No one knew exactly how old she was—not even her—but it was agreed she was more than a hundred. Her skin was a deep, dark chocolate colour, and her hands small and nimble. I remember playing with her hands, stroking and pulling at the veins that popped out and snaked around the backs of them. She had tattoos inked into her skin, markings with a meaning I still do not understand. She could thread a needle still, she didn't wear glasses, and she had a sweet tooth to rival anyone's—she loved hard, boiled lollies especially, and would unwrap them gleefully and pop them into her mouth. She was well loved by everyone in the family. She was very active, although she needed help walking; but there was never any shortage of people to hold on to her hand as she made her way around, whether it was to get from room to room, house to house, or to the 'tolek', as she called the bathroom.

My Aaja's land on Malolo Street was dotted by mango trees of many varieties, and every mango season, Fua Aaji would make massive amounts of mango achar, or pickles. Fua Aaji oversaw the picking, washing and cutting of piles of unripe mangoes. Before they could be pickled, they had to be dried; Fua Aaji would lay the cut pieces of mango on sheets of corrugated iron propped up by empty forty-four gallon drums in the clearing between the two blocks of flats. When the mango pieces had been in the hot sun for a couple of days, they would shrivel slightly, the gleaming wetness of the cut flesh sapped by the sun; my cousins and I were drawn to these warm wedges of intense sweet-and-sour mango, despite the abundance of fresh fruit hanging from the surrounding trees. We would steal handfuls of wedges and run, Fua Aaji yelling at us from her balcony. Ram Ram Aajia would always come to our defence, scolding her daughter, and encouraging us to grab a few more handfuls before we scurried away to scoff them.

When I left Fiji in 1991, I was sad to leave Ram Ram Aajia. I had a feeling I'd not see her again, and that she would go and I would not be able to make it back for her funeral. A few years afterwards, that's exactly what happened, and I mourned her from my home in Melbourne. Afterwards, I heard stories of her funeral, attended by hundreds of people, and of my father and his brothers clutching at each other and howling for the loss of their grandmother.

Then one night I had a dream. I woke up to find her sitting at the end of my bed. She smiled at me as I sat up. We hugged, and I buried my face in the nape of her neck, inhaling her powdery, musty, comforting scent as we both cried. When I woke, my cheeks and pillow were wet with tears, but a sense of calm surrounded me. I believe it really was her, my Ram Ram Aajia, and am thankful we finally got to say goodbye to each other.

I HAD TWO PATERNAL GRANDMOTHERS, or Aajis. My father's mother passed away when I was two years old, but not too soon to see her husband, my Aaja, bring another wife into her home. My Aaja and Aaji had nine children at that stage; Aaji was pregnant with their tenth. Given my Aaji's ailing health (she had been coughing up blood, and was thought to be suffering tuberculosis), in an apparently mutual decision between husband and wife it was decided that Aaja would take a new wife to help look after his children when my Aaji was gone. Aaja went to India to find his second wife; he chose a bit-part Bollywood actress. My father has never referred to his father's new wife as his mother; instead, he calls her Mausi, a term which means 'an aunt who is my mother's sister'.

I'd seen pictures in old photo albums of both my Aaja's wives together—my father's mother dressed in plain saris and minimal jewellery, in stark contrast to the flamboyance of my Aaja's new wife. She was always dressed to impress in rich silk saris with matching blouses, laden with intricate gold jewellery, and her kohl-lined eyes always glittered; she seemed perpetually on the verge of laughter.

I remember one time at my uncle's house on the top floor of the double-storey block of flats, watching a videotape of a Bollywood movie she had 'starred' in. It was black and white. She was quite plainly dressed—her hair was twisted into a bun, and her sari was not patterned—I guess so as not to draw undue attention away from the main characters. Even so, I thought she was extremely glamorous. I watched as she walked into the scene and spoke one, maybe two lines, and walked out again.

Sitting on the floor in my uncle's darkened lounge room that night surrounded by my cousins, the room filled with excited chatter, I remember her tinkling laugh as I looked from the picture on the screen back to her. My father's mother was there too, in a way. A large framed photograph of my first Aaji stared down at all of us from one of the lounge-room walls. It had been there for at least five years, wreathed in a fragile-looking, papery garland—the mark of the departed.

INSTEAD OF IN THE BRANCHES of the family tree we drew earlier, Drasa Naani would be found seated in the shade underneath it. Although she isn't actually related to me, Drasa Naani has been in my life for as long as I can remember. And before that she was a fixture in my father's life, from well before he was married. Her husband had been a long-time employee of my Aaja's, and she was connected to our family so closely that she might as well have been part of it.

Drasa Naani lived in a village called Drasa, where my Aaja owned property and where my father went on to build our farmhouse when I was fourteen. We would visit her house some weekends, before we'd moved to the area. When my father built our house in Drasa, we became neighbours—she lived with her husband, daughter, two sons, one daughter-in-law and three grandchildren in a lean-to, corrugated iron shack in the valley at front end of our property. While our house was being built, Drasa Naani's husband spent nights in the foreman's shack on the building site. When the house was finished and we moved in, we took Drasa Naani on as an employee. Every morning, she would walk up the sloping driveway and spend the day at the house while we went to school and work. She would keep the house in our absence, cleaning and dusting, putting clothes out and bringing them in off the line, keeping houseguests like Naani and Ram Ram Aajia company whenever they came over to stay.

Drasa Naani is not like my other grandmothers; she is short and compact, lean from years of working with her hands. She would give me warm coconut oil head massages when I felt like some pampering, and gave the best backrubs. She was there when my brother was suddenly taken ill, and she rubbed a brass vessel called a lota on the soles of his feet to draw out his fever. She was there when I came home from school in the middle of the day, flushed and embarrassed at having gotten my first period. She was there too when my oldest brother had his first child in Melbourne, sent by my parents for support in their absence. Drasa Naani has been there so much for our family that I'd often wonder if that had ever affected her relationship with her own.

The last time I saw Drasa Naani was when I visited Fiji in 2004. We dropped in at her place on the way back from visiting the farmhouse we used to live in on the hilltop, and that lingering question was answered the second I walked into her house. Together with pictures of her own family, the walls of the front room were adorned with framed pictures of my family: my nephew's posed school photos, snaps from the snow trip we made when Drasa Naani was in Melbourne, random images that Naani had captured and treasured, and now gazed at every day. Our families, though not related through blood, would always be intertwined in both our hearts and homes.

FOUR GRANDMOTHERS out of many, and I'd never really sat down to focus on the nature of my relationships with any of them before, never really analysed this part of my family life. I realise now, however, that although I love them all in different ways, I have never really felt an extreme closeness with any of them. So although I never had the 'traditional', grandmotherly, apple-pie-baking and sleep-overs relationship, I have been blessed with so many memories, thanks to my many, many grandmothers.

The Tyranny of Distance

JULIE McCROSSIN

MY ENGLISH GRANDMOTHER drove an ambulance during the London Blitz. I don't remember when I first heard this story about Nana, my mother's mother, Florence Hedges. But I do know I grew up loving the idea that a woman could be out on the city streets, driving an ambulance in a blackout, as the Nazi bombs fell on London.

The purpose of the Blitz was to demoralise the civilian population and force the British government to stop fighting the Nazis. The bombing lasted from 7 September 1940 to 11 May 1941. However, it wasn't just London that took a beating. Bombs blasted other cities all over Britain as well. But it was London that suffered most frequently. At one stage the city experienced fifty-seven consecutive days of intense bombing. An estimated 177,000 people sheltered in the London underground each night, including, at times, Nana, my grandfather, Arthur Bertie Hedges, and their two teenage daughters, Ivy and Marjorie, my mother.

The relentless bombing created terrible fires. On 29 December 1940, they were so numerous and intense, the blaze was called the 'Second Great Fire of London'. Ernie Pyle, a leading journalist of the day who witnessed the Blitz, famously described a night raid over London. It was not the great fire night, just an average night during the Blitz, 'when London was ringed and stabbed with fire'.

> You have seen big fires, but I doubt if you have ever seen the whole horizon of a city lined with great fires—scores of them, perhaps hundreds. There was something inspiring in just the awful savagery of it. Flames seemed to whip hundreds of feet into the air.

Pyle also witnessed the frantic attempts of the Londoners to put out the incendiary bombs. 'These white points would go out one by one,' he wrote, 'as the unseen heroes of the moment smothered them with sand.'

On these terrible nights, my grandmother and grandfather were among those Londoners scrambling to save their city and their lives. By the end of the Blitz 51,509 civilians had died. In London alone, over a million homes had been destroyed or damaged. Two of them were where my family lived.

The first family home that was bombed was in Watney Road, East Sheen. It was destroyed completely. My mother remembers getting into the shelter that her father had dug at the bottom of the garden. Luckily he'd dug it a long way from the house and he'd surrounded it with crates full of rubble to protect it from any blast. Grandad had seen action in World War I and he knew what bombs could do. The night the house was destroyed, the whole family, including the border collie Pete, was buried alive. They had to be dug out.

After this, as my mother remembers it, they spent many nights sleeping in warehouses down by the Thames, on concrete floors under grey blankets. From there, Nana would go off each evening to drive her ambulance, while Grandad would work as a driver for the police during the day and as an air raid warden at night, sometimes digging other people out of the rubble. My mother and her sister, then in their mid teens, spent many nights without their parents during the Blitz.

The second family home to be bombed was in Ormond Road, East Sheen. Thankfully it didn't take a direct hit. Mum remembers that the bomb hit the house 'next door but one'. But the blast was strong enough to take out a wall from Nana's house. This time they'd been lucky. But the dog had to be moved elsewhere. He couldn't stand the sound of the bombs after that.

WHENEVER MY MOTHER SPEAKS about Nana's war service, she always tells the story of Nana's first night out in the ambulance. It was with a team of women and a doctor. A bomb had fallen on a building in Brixton and eighty people were killed.

'God knows how many more were injured,' my mother says. 'Nana and the women had to pull the bodies out. They'd also been trained to give first aid to the living.'

According to Mum's version of events, Nana spoke freely to her family about what happened on that first night in Brixton, but after that, she never spoke about her wartime ambulance experiences again.

'She could be nervy in later life and you can hardly wonder why,' my mother explains. 'She did a fantastic job.'

Many years later, growing up as a teenager in the late 1960s and early 1970s in Australia, I became an active 'women's libber'. I don't know if there was a direct connection between my passionate feminism and the stories I'd heard about Nana. But I do know that I developed a conviction that women could do anything they set their minds to and that all barriers to equality just had to be kicked out of the way.

A lot of feminists got excited in 1980 when a US documentary film, entitled *The Life and Times of Rosie the Riveter*, came to Australia. It was about the non-traditional jobs women did during World War II, so the men could go to war. It was full of footage of women working in heavy industry and driving large machinery. It worked like rocket fuel at the time, encouraging the agitation of the period for 'men's jobs' (and their pay scales) to be opened up for women. But it felt like old news to me. I'd grown up hearing about Nana in the Blitz and seeing pictures of women in uniform doing 'men's work'. I was surprised how few people in Australia knew about the active role that women played during World War II. It was the first time I realised how important it is to pass on the stories.

MY NANA wasn't the only woman in my family to see uniformed service during wartime. My grandfather's sister, Ivy, was killed in World War I, while working as a nurse in the trenches. My mother joined the WAAF, the Women's Auxiliary Air Force, in 1942 when she was only seventeen and a half. Her younger sister, Ivy, (named no doubt after her brave aunt) followed her into the services eighteen months later.

But Mum and Ivy were just two of the thousands of women who joined the WAAF after war broke out. My mother says every able-bodied person between seventeen and about forty-four was expected to support the war effort. Many women were called up. Others volunteered well before the call-up notice came. Between 1939 and 1945, the number of women in the WAAF increased from 8,800 to 153,000.

Aunty Ivy worked in administration. Mum worked in operations and signals at air bases across southern Britain. At one stage, she was stationed at a RAF base called Little Staughton in Huntingdonshire, as part of Bomber Command, and it was here she met a handsome Australian Pathfinder pilot called Robert McCrossin. Mum and Dad were married in uniform and Mum sailed out to Australia on a ship full of brides when the war was over.

Of course, the men in my family went to war as well. My grandfather, Nana's husband and my mother's beloved father, was in the trenches of the Great War at the age of sixteen and a half. His brother Wilfred was in the trenches too. His father, my great-grandfather, was at the Boer War. Nana's brother Ron was in the British Army and her brother Dennis in the British Air Force, during World War II. And, of course, there is my father's side of the family as well. My paternal grandfather, Hubert, fought on the Western Front in the First War and my father's brother, Dick, was in the navy in the Second. I won't get started on the extended family. Our family albums are full of photographs of people in uniform.

Now in later life, I have become increasingly keen to learn about my father's experiences as a Lancaster Bomber pilot in the Pathfinders, an elite squadron in Bomber Command, which played a crucial role in the main attacks on German cities and installations. It is one of the complexities of my family story that we were on both the receiving and the delivery ends of the bombing raids of World War II. When you walk into the Australian War Memorial in Canberra, there is a photo on the wall of a squadron of men surrounding a Lancaster Bomber. My dad is in that photograph.

Yet somehow, as a young girl, in the midst of all these stories of courage and duty, it was Nana's story that inspired me the most. It is the image of my brave maternal grandmother driving ambulances in the Blitz that stood out in my youthful imagination.

Perhaps I was hungry at that early stage of my life for proof that girls could do anything. And certainly my mother's stories about wartime London created a vivid picture in my mind of the terrible danger raining down on Nana and her team as day after day she drove her ambulance through the debris-strewn streets. Even now, my mother can readily list the different types of bombs the family experienced: the V-1 flying bombs, the V-2 rockets, the Doodlebugs and the Molotov Baskets. 'There were flying bombs with a light on them and when the light went off, they came down, and the Molotov Baskets illuminated us,' she says. 'I was terrified.'

MY NANA'S full name was Florence Helen Hedges. Her maiden name was Mardlin. She was brought up on Newman's Farm near Harlington, with her mother, Nana Frances and her father, Mr Mardlin. Nana Frances married a second time to Mr Burrows and had two sons, my Nana's half brothers, Ron and Dennis. But it seems Mr Burrows ill-treated my Nana in some way and so she came to London with her mother and they lived for a while with a Baptist minister.

I really only got to know my Nana properly when I made my first trip to Britain in the early 1970s at the age of twenty. All those years down the track, the Baptist influence was still there in the woman I met. Nana loved a smoke and a drink, but she always gave up both for Lent.

My grandmother visited Australia seven times during my upbringing. But most of these visits were either before I was born, or when I was too small to remember them. My mother had several bouts of serious illness that took her away to hospital for many months at a time. So Nana would come out by boat, making the long trip from London to Sydney, through the Suez Canal, to help with us five children—my two big brothers Bobbie and Ian, my two little sisters, Fiona and Lindy, and of course me.

There was one trip she made when I was in high school. I should be able to remember that visit, but I don't. My memories of it are foggy. So my first crystal clear recollection of Nana is when she came to meet me at the Brighton bus terminal, south of London. I enjoyed her immensely from the first moment.

NANA WAS A DYNAMIC, funny, energetic woman. She was a Londoner who spoke with a working class accent. She would sometimes let her cigarette hang from her mouth. The ash would get very long and occasionally drop onto her chest. She was always well dressed and carefully groomed, which made this casual approach to cigarette ash even more noticeable.

She lived in a remarkably beautiful, small village called Poynings, five miles north-west of Brighton, on the north side of the South Downs, near a big, long hill called the Devil's Dyke. Her home was a tiny cottage behind a classic, country pub called The Royal Oak. The cottage was very small and hundreds of years old. Standing up, I could place the palms of my hands flat on the ceiling and I am a short woman. Nana's toilet was 'up the garden'. The water in the toilet froze during winter and there was ice on the inside of the window panes in the tiny upstairs bedroom where I slept. In spring, her garden was full of flowers and she also had an allotment nearby where she grew fresh vegetables. The tomatoes grown in Nana's glasshouse were the best I've ever eaten.

This little cottage was known as a Watneys widow's cottage. My grandfather had a stroke while working very long hours for the brewer, Watneys. As an employee, he'd been given the cottage for use during his lifetime and this is where he died, before I had a chance to meet him, which remains a source of great sadness to me. Under the agreement with Watneys, Nana had the use of the cottage until her own death in 1986 at the age of eighty-seven.

I visited Nana in this beautiful place several times, but sadly it was not often enough. In his famous book, *The Tyranny of Distance*, the Australian historian Geoffrey Blainey wrote about how distance has shaped our national identity and institutions. The title of his work still resonates with me as I reflect on my family's history. Poynings is a long way from Australia and to this day my mother carries the burden of having never seen her father again after he waved her goodbye at the end of the war.

Yet despite the physical distance between my Nana and I when she was alive, and the infrequent contact, I continue to feel a strong connection to my Nana. My working life has been dominated by the media and performance. Nana loved news and current affairs and always listened to the BBC. I was in her lounge room as the approval of the impeachment of President Nixon unfolded and we debated the issues with energy. When the Poynings parish church of the Holy Trinity, which dates back to 1087 on that site, celebrated a major anniversary, Nana played seven roles in the village pageant. One of the locals who helped with direction was Talbot Rothwell, the writer of the *Carry On* movies, who lived in a nearby village. Nana introduced me to him one day and we shared some very lively conversations.

I feel a connection to Nana as a working woman as well. After the war, when she was no longer required to drive the

Buick ambulance supplied by the Americans, she worked for a while as the driver of a Rolls Royce for a rich, elderly lady called Miss Scarlett and her small dogs. Perhaps I've inherited Nana's capacity behind the wheel. When I was a young performer in a children's theatre company called Pipi Storm in the late 1970s, I took six months off from acting and became a government bus driver in Sydney. And I still love driving, especially big things, and I like to think this is an ongoing link to my grandmother.

IN HER SEVENTIES Nana got a new job. She was bored, and so she found work as a housekeeper at a police college in Hove. When the village bus service was cut, she continued to walk about thirty minutes to the crossroads to pick up a bus, no small feat for an elderly woman in inclement British weather.

Nana and I shared a great love of dogs as well, and this would become one of the reasons we didn't see much of her in Sydney as she grew older. Nana acquired a small, apricot poodle called Pebbles and, as she couldn't bear to leave her dog behind, she stopped making trips to Australia. From then on, we had to visit her in Poynings.

In her later life, Nana developed heart problems. One Thursday, my mother was talking to her on a long distance telephone call. Nana told Mum that a nurse was coming to put dressings on her leg, which had ulcers. Then, she said, she was going to the vet's to have Pebbles put down, and after that she'd go to the hospital. My mother started crying because Nana had always said that if she felt she was going to die she would have Pebbles put down.

Everything subsequently happened just as Nana had always said it would. She had Pebbles put down. Then she went to the hospital. She died the following Tuesday. For my immigrant mother, it was another acute experience of the tyranny of distance. It was for us children as well.

I remember so well the last time I waved Nana goodbye in Poynings. She was standing in her garden and I think we both knew it was probably the last time we'd see each other. I cried as I walked to the crossroads to pick up the bus, just as I am crying now.

Looking for Love

EILEEN NASEBY

IT WAS THE SUMMER of that old rented cottage on Cleveland Point.

It was 1959, the year television was first broadcast in Brisbane, but only to those residents who could afford a television set, which we couldn't; Billy Graham came to town and converted my future husband's first father-in-law; the population of Australia reached ten million. All these things happened without my noticing. I had just turned sixteen and had no interest in anything that was not directly useful to me. For 1959 was the year I first fell in love, and found my first job, at the university on the other side of the city. It was also the year I tasted my first breath of adult freedom, being allowed to stay at a Girls Friendly Society hostel during the week to save the long hours of travel to and from work. There is another reason why the summer of 1959 was so memorable; it was the first time my grandmother ever talked to me about men and love, subjects no one in our family had ever discussed before.

Cleveland Point jutted out from the mainland like a thin dagger. My grandmother and I were going for a walk from the cottage to the lighthouse which stood at the end of the peninsula. The tide was almost out, and the great muddy expanse of Moreton Bay lay exposed before us like a dark brown amoeba drying out under a hot blue sky. Gulls wheeled and shrieked across the still-moist sand that writhed with the frenzy of millions of hidden sea creatures. Instead of taking my grandmother along the road I had made her climb down from the sea wall so we could walk along the edge of the mudflats. As I watched her nervously picking her way around craggy rocks and puddles of seawater I was reminded that a large part of our relationship was based on my callousness and her compliance. In her suede cork-heeled shoes and nylon stockings she was forced to keep stopping as she tried to pick out the best spot for her next footstep to land. As a mark of my brutality I skipped ahead in my sandshoes to show her how clever I was to be young.

Sometimes I turned and called to her, 'Mama, you're too slow!' Mama was what we all called her, even my dad Nigel.

Mama kept answering me, 'So what's the hurry?'

I loved my grandmother but sometimes she drove me crazy. All weekend she had been getting under my skin. Only that morning she'd tried to steal some photos of my father from my mother's wooden box of photographs, photos that were no business of anyone else but my mother and me. If I hadn't made her give them back she would have destroyed them for sure. I'd been made to help her sort out the removal boxes in the storeroom at the front of the house. The room was a mess, because everybody else had been digging into the boxes to get at their stuff while I was at work.

There were only four of us children then—my sisters Diana and Charmian, my six-year-old baby brother Stephen and me. We had been in the house on Cleveland Point for less than a month. I resented having to spend my weekends unpacking other people's stuff when I was the one who was at work all week. My mother was spending most of her time in bed. As the eldest, the biggest responsibility fell on my shoulders. On the other hand, my grandmother loved creating order out of our family messes; the bigger the mess, the higher she rose to each occasion. Being a clumsy clot I had simply let the box of photographs slip out of my hands and Mama, sighing with exasperation, knelt awkwardly to help me pick up the fallen photos. As she bent forward I caught a whiff of her signature perfume, cigarette smoke mixed with the fragrance of her home-made moisturising cream, a concoction she made from a lanoline base, a recipe she had come across in her travels, which she mixed up in large bowls in her tiny kitchen. She called the cream *Charmian* after my sister, and had someone print up professional labels. One day she hoped to make us all rich. One day she would be as famous as Helena Rubenstein. I heard her mutter something under her breath.

'What? What?' I raised my voice to her.

She put her hand behind her back as she stood up to hide a photo she was holding.

'Let me see,' I demanded.

'It's nothing,' she replied.

'Nussink, what do you mean nussink? Mama, if it's nussink then why won't you let me look?'

'It's just your father.'

I danced behind her and whipped the photo out of her grasp.

'My father? It's not my father.'

And then I realised who she meant. The picture was of my real father, Tony Piercy, not my stepfather Nigel Hall who I have always thought of as my father even though I knew he wasn't. Posing beside Tony was my very young and beautiful mother holding me in her arms. It was a professional photograph, taken in Haifa in Palestine when I was just a few weeks old. It was plain to see we were not a happy little family, even then. A few months later my mother would leave Tony and, except for a brief visit to our flat in London when I was four, I would have no contact with him until I reached middle age.

'I don't understand why I've never seen this photo before,' I said to my grandmother who was now scrabbling through the box to see if she could find any more photos of my father.

She found another one that I had seen before. I insisted on looking at it. It was a head and shoulders portrait of my mother and Tony. She was leaning on his shoulder, looking as beautiful as ever. Tony was very neat, but there was something odd about his hooded eyes and his slick moustache that made him look quite creepy.

Mama suddenly snatched this photograph out of my hand and pushed them both into her apron pocket, which is when I grabbed her wrist and took both photos back. I stalked off into the house to confront my mother about keeping the photographs of my father a secret from me.

I returned five minutes later, chastened by my mother's accusation that I was the only one she knew who could manufacture dramas out of thin air. I could see the rigid structure of Mama's face had collapsed into rubbery lines as if she was about to cry.

'What's wrong with you now?' I demanded, taking out my anger with my mother on her.

'I am in fear for your future.'

'Fear for my future? Don't be ridiculous, Mama!'

'I don't want you making the same mistakes as your mother.'

'What mistakes?'

'Each man she has chosen has been the wrong one.'

'Zee wrong vun?' I teased. 'What about Daddy? Is he zee wrong vun too?'

'Yes he has his good points,' she conceded. 'I would agree with this, but he is not so good a provider.'

'But he loves her. She loves him. Isn't that all that matters?'

'Your mother could have had anything she ever wanted. She has such enormous intelligence. So what good has it been to her? Can't you see how she is living? At least if she had stayed with your father, with Tony, she would not have such money worries. Has your mother ever told you your father's family was very wealthy? His great-grandfather made a huge fortune out of building railways all over the world. Your father used to say his family owned half of the island of Sardinia.'

Of course what I discovered when I finally met my father in 1986 was that he really was the fabricator my mother had always said he was. That part of the family fortune left to Tony's father and his sister Vera by their father, had been lost long before he met my mother. My grandfather and great-aunt had allowed her husband, Count Francesco Giorgio di Mameli Oristano, Italian Ambassador to the Holy See, to manage their considerable inheritance which he quickly lost through reckless investments in risky endeavours.

I was looking at my grandmother with amazement. I had to think for a moment before I answered. 'So you're saying that she should have stayed with Tony even though he was cruel to her, just because he had a lot of money?'

She shrugged her shoulders without answering.

I was shocked. Despite all our family problems, especially my arguments with my mother, what had always held us all together was my parents' deep and obvious love of one another. To have their beautiful relationship described as something negative, and on top of this to criticise my beloved stepfather for his shortcomings, was more than I could bear.

I screamed at her. 'Mama, don't you ever say such horrible things about my parents again.'

My parents were poor. Nigel was intelligent but he hadn't been able to get a decent job since we arrived in Australia from England in 1952. He had spent his early years as a policeman, first in London and then in the British Mounted Police force in Palestine where he met my mother. Nigel loved horses and his dream was to one day have his own horse stud. His first job in Australia was on a large station on the Darling Downs, but something happened between him and his boss, and eventually we ended up coming to live in Brisbane. Now we were on a waiting list for Housing Commission accommodation.

In the meantime Nigel had rented this little cottage a long way from the city because it was all they could afford. My mother had only recently returned home to Brisbane after spending six months in a Sydney hospital recovering from a hip replacement operation which my grandmother had paid for. In 1934, when my mother was ten she had caught diphtheria in the refugee camp in Palestine where she and my grandmother were placed when they arrived as illegal immigrants from Germany. The disease, which paralysed her for several weeks, also left her with a nasty bone disease that had gradually eaten away at her hip and its socket.

Mama's frugality was legendary. Although her father had trained her as a watchmaker, circumstances had led my grandmother to work all her life in restaurants or for catering companies. Never highly paid, she still managed to pull thousands of pounds out of a hat whenever my parents had a financial or medical crisis, which was quite often. She was a champion scrimper and saver, often taking home our stale bread to eat for herself. She drove us all crazy with her criticisms of the amount of food we wasted.

MY MOTHER had hardly left her bed since the day we arrived at Cleveland Point. Mama spent most of her time, as she did whenever she stayed with us, hovering in the hall beside my mother's bedroom, listening for signs of her discomfort so she could minister to her every need. No matter how badly she was treated by my mother, Mama still kept looking after her daughter as if nothing had happened. Sometimes they fought; my mother said she hated my grandmother's martyrdom, and my grandmother felt hurt and angry, but their fights were always in German so we never really understood what they were screaming at each other.

After lunch I found Mama standing in front of the living room window, watching a storm that had climbed up over North Straddie. A tall rainbow blazed out of the dark blue clouds lighting up a tiny old fishing boat, far out in the bay, so it glowed like a glorious beacon. I searched my grandmother's face for signs she was enjoying the spectacle, but when she realised she was being watched, she pulled her dry lips down into her jaw line. Deep violet creases around her chin framed her disapproval. Later in the afternoon, after we had emptied most of the boxes, I realised the tide had gone out and I begged her to come for a walk. Eventually she caved in but she refused to take off her stockings and her good shoes.

Some of Mama's clothes had been made by a tailor in Germany before she left Europe with my mother in 1933. She boasted all the time about the quality of her 'costumes', as she called her suits, telling us that only in Europe would we ever be able to find such quality. They were beautifully preserved because she treated them as precious possessions, always hanging them inside out in men's calico suit covers with camphor balls to protect them from moths. She used shoe trees in all her shoes and put each pair inside old stockings to protect them when she wasn't wearing them.

The tide was a long way out, but still Mama clucked and shuddered at the thought of being so close to the water. I wanted to show her everything I had discovered since we arrived—oyster shell-encrusted rocks scattered casually on the uncovered seabed, miniature crabs scurrying from one hidey hole to another with minuscule loads of sand, and sometimes little shoals of tiny fish marooned in tidal puddles. But her reaction was always a look of distaste. In the end I tried distracting her by pestering her for romantic stories about my grandfather who lived in Germany and whom I had never met because he and Mama were divorced when my mother was just a little girl. She never wanted to talk about her ex-husband. It was as if she was embarrassed to have married him. My mother said her father was a nice person, but not very bright, which was the opposite of my grandmother, who taught herself to speak English by translating Shakespeare's plays from German.

'Was he very handsome, Solomon?' I asked. 'Was he very rich?'

She shrugged her shoulders. 'He was a man. Not so special.'

'Did you love him?'

She stood still. 'Listen! This is what I mean. I am telling you there is nothing to be had in this love business.'

'What is wrong with love?'

She shook her head very slowly with frustration. 'What I am trying to tell you is very important. You should listen good. It is a big mistake to marry for this dream of love. Security is what must come first, then if you are very lucky, then maybe love might even happen, and then you have the best of both worlds.'

I jumped up onto the sea wall and sat down, banging my heels against the sandstone.

'My friend Jan and I have already worked out what sort of men we're going to marry. I would like to marry a vet, someone who likes animals. I keep thinking he would wear one of those jackets with leather in the sleeves.'

'So! This is what I mean. Already your head is filled with such rubbish.' She reached stiffly for a tiny piece of driftwood.

This was my very favourite subject so I ploughed on regardless. 'Do you want to know what else?'

'If you are big enough to have such ideas then you should know there are dangers waiting for you. You don't understand about this business with men? It is too easy to end up with a baby. You know what I am saying?'

I banged my heels even faster against the wall, twisting up my mouth, and rolling my eyes with mock embarrassment.

'An unwanted baby is a terrible burden …' Mama stopped short and gave me a pained look.

'What do you mean, baby?' I giggled.

She continued. Her voice was now low and grave with the weight of what she was about to say. 'It happened to my friend. During the war she went with a man because she needed someone to protect her. She thought it was love. Who knows what it was in those times?'

I sat up and paid attention to the word, love.

'Later the man was killed. My friend went to a doctor when she found she was having a baby. She had no choice. It was what many women had to do. Who would bring a baby into a world of such death and destruction? The doctor made an operation to take the baby away before it was born.'

A breeze from the north was ruffling Mama's grey hair. The air had become moist and was filled with the crying of seagulls. My grandmother was never one to read us fairy stories, not even the Grimm Brothers, but she had a competitive store of her own, wild crazy tales of disappearance, death and imprisonment. Only in her stories there were no soft landings, no heroes ever arrived to rescue her sisters—the ballerina Tamara who disappeared in Sarajevo, or Miriam who died in the Warsaw uprising. And I knew this story was also going to end in disaster. I scrunched my shoulders into my ears to disguise a shiver, but Mama saw anyway and knew I was still listening.

'Many years later I met my friend's cousin. I worked with him in King David Hotel in Jerusalem. He told me Leila had married a nice man after the war, and they had a little girl. She was so happy at last, but then the child died in her sleep. Leila went crazy. She thought God had punished her for what she had done. Her husband had to put her in a lunatic asylum.'

Mama stopped walking and turned to face me and I immediately looked down at my feet. It was what I always did when my mother or my grandmother talked about the terrible times before I was born. She turned away, looking out across the rippled surface of the muddy sand to where Stradbroke Island rolled softly along the horizon. She seemed even smaller than usual, her square black dress set against the sad flow of her shoulders.

What had all this talk of dead babies to do with me, I wondered.

I would have liked to put my arms around her, but we didn't do this in our family. We didn't touch each other. The closest my grandmother came to displaying physical affection to any of her grandchildren was by vigorously cleaning our faces with a handkerchief that she had first wetted with her tongue.

So instead I yelled at her, 'Mama, why is it you always talk such rubbish? You ruin everything! Why can't you talk like an ordinary grandmother? Why can't you learn to speak English properly?'

Towards the horizon I could see Harold, who lived right under the lighthouse, sending his Flying Dutchman scudding across the blue shallows. I wished I was out on the bay with my shy sweet sailor boy who had taken me sailing for the first time only the week before. Our romance was not destined to last for very long, but at this moment I thought it would be forever. I jumped from the wall, spurting mud and salty water over Mama's immaculate stockings and cork heels.

'You are so naughty!' Mama said.

But in her eyes I already caught the soft brown light of forgiveness, and I asked myself once again why she kept putting up with all the stuff that was dished up to her. Somehow I just couldn't help copying my mother, even though I knew only too well the grief it caused my grandmother, because my mother's bad temper caused me so much suffering as well.

EIGHTEEN MONTHS LATER Jan and I were discussing my grandmother's instructions regarding men and babies. We were doing my mother's ironing in the kitchen of the Housing Commission house in Inala. My parents had gone to visit friends, taking my new baby sister Naomi with them. Jan was holding a Craven A unfiltered cigarette precariously between her lips. She delicately picked tiny tobacco pieces off the end of her tongue, at the same time trying to suppress a cough.

'It's because of what happened in the war,' I said. 'That's why my grandmother goes on about those things. It's because my mother screams at her all the time and blames her. Sometimes I hate my mother.'

'Your mother is so beautiful,' said Jan, shaking one of

Nigel's shirts across the ironing board. 'And she's a great reader. You should never hate your mother.'

Then I told Jan that my grandmother had been trying to match-make me with a Jewish boy from work. She had asked me to go with her to the synagogue. I was very surprised. I had no idea she was even still attached to the Jewish religion. After the service she wanted to take me to meet the Rabbi. I just assumed she wanted to show off her eldest grandchild. How wrong I was. We went into his little office and sat down. After my grandmother introduced me, there was a bit of small talk, and then, out of the blue, Rabbi Fabian asked me about Isaac Levy. I must have looked flabbergasted because I saw a look of concern pass between Mama and the Rabbi.

Isaac was a junior lecturer in the university where I worked as a museum assistant and considerably older than me. He was a tall, gangly, shy young man with bad breath and a penchant for heavy petting. The Rabbi began raving about Isaac's virtues—handsome, reliable, would be very well off one day and a good religious boy. For a moment I wondered if he was talking about the same person. I had only been out with Isaac twice. The first time he was such a perfect gentleman, even my parents would have approved. But on the second date I was only narrowly saved from rape by the timely intervention of a member of the local constabulary who was patrolling the lovers' lane where Isaac had insisted on driving me.

My grandmother's conversation with me that day in Cleveland Point came flooding back. What was she up to? I was staring hard at her and her co-conspirator, wondering how they could possibly be serious, but they were. In the next breath the Rabbi told me that Isaac was considering proposing to me. So they had been talking to him as well! I couldn't believe I had been cornered like this. Mama's face was full of hope as she waited for my response. I realised I couldn't embarrass her by telling them the truth—that I would never marry Isaac Levy even if he was the last man on earth. So I told a white lie and said I'd think about it.

Jan thought my story was very funny.

'You'll have to tell them,' she said. 'Otherwise you'll never get them off your back, especially Isaac.'

I was listening to her. She was the older one by eighteen months, and far more stable than me. I had learned so much from her since we had become friends. The first thing she did was to teach me how to dress. I deferred to Jan in all matters of taste because she always looked so elegant and read *Seventeen* magazine from America, a glossy instruction of good fashion. That night we were going into the city and I was going to wear the turquoise blue linen skirt she had made for my eighteenth birthday.

'Oh Eil!' she would say, more often than not when I bought something new. 'You can't wear that pattern, it isn't very flattering.'

When we had finished the ironing we caught the train to Brisbane. We were going to the cinema. I carried the white bag Jan had picked out for me in Cahill's shoe shop. It didn't smell like the real leather of Mama's handbags. Still, it looked like the real thing and it matched the thin-heeled shoes with the little white bows that flashed under the neon signs as we made our way down Queen Street. I made sure my elbow was bent across my waist so the handle of my bag was wedged tight into the crook of my arm. Click, click went our heels on the pavement, white bags and white gloves flashing to each other as we sauntered and talked. To the watchers in the pubs and on the footpaths we were young women of confidence, mouthing our red lips into the burnished light of the early evening. I had entered into a vibrant new world a thousand miles from home. No one in my family could reach me here, not even my grandmother with her stern commandments.

I was looking for love.

Show Me, She Said

ANNE DEVESON

Sleeping over at Grandma Anne's by Odessa Blain, aged 9

GRANDMAS, THEY ARE USEFUL for lots of things, mainly fun. They are not as close as parents, but they are one of the inner parts of our family. They have weird little things that they are quite touchy about, and weird little habits.

A normal sleepover at my grandma's house has a couple of rules. Firstly, we would have to play Monopoly. My mum and grandma are on the computer all the time, talking about real estate. My grandma, ever since I was born, was talking about moving. She normally says stuff like would we all like to move to a horse farm. And we never do. Once mum, dad, a friend and I were playing Monopoly. Our friend was doing horribly. Eventually she left because she had to go home. My grandma took over. She looked at our friend's property and said, 'I am mortgaging those, selling them.' Within ten minutes she was back in the game!!

Every sleepover we discover new things about each other. For example once I discovered she is very touchy about grammar. You can only say 'aitch', not 'haitch'. And you cannot say, 'Can I have them?' You are meant to say, 'May I have the biscuits please?' She says you have to use good grammar to look educated.

Every time I go to her house we normally have roast chicken for dinner, followed by dessert that she always calls pudding because she's English. So I always think we're having pudding for dessert and I get greatly surprised when a delicious bowl of chocolate mousse is on the table.

In the morning I wake up and I hear some loud classical music coming from my grandma's room. So I totter down the hall and have a peep. She is lying in bed all cosy, reading the newspaper, sipping casually at a cup of tea.

So I come to a conclusion that the world would be empty without grandmas and their weird little habits. There would be no fun in the world. I reckon grandmas make the world go round.

ONE WINTER'S MORNING when I was getting dressed, my four-year-old grand-daughter stared at me. She stared at my face. She stared at my bare arms. She stared at my legs. She stared and stared. Then she spoke.

'Are you wrinkled *all over*?' she asked.

'No,' I said, trying not to sound indignant.

She was unimpressed. Her eyes narrowed.

'*Show me*,' she said.

And that, I realised, is one of the delights of being a grandparent. One outrageously honest question about wrinkles, one early morning leap into bed with youthful energy and enthusiasm, one bear hug, even one tantrum, can take you back to that time when the years stretched endlessly ahead as you helter-skeltered through the scary and exquisite pleasure of being a parent. There were also the agonies. The childhood tantrums that turned into teenage rebellion, the endless meals that needed cooking, the time that was required, the responsibility. Which is possibly why Gore Vidal once pronounced: 'Never have children, only grandchildren.'

Well, I have three grandchildren, just as once I had three children. Two of my grandchildren, Bronte and Brodie, aged twelve and eleven live on the Sunshine Coast. The third, Odessa, lives in Sydney. She is ten. I see more of her than the others but whenever there's a chance to bring the three cousins together, we make it happen.

I also have eleven step grandchildren and three step great-grandchildren. I can look behind me a long way, and I can still look ahead.

Being a grandparent is a mysterious process. For me, it's pleasure all the way, but underlying the surface there is something deeper than pleasure. It's that messy mysterious cobweb of family, that may seem fragile, yet test it, call upon it, and mostly it is steely strong. If my grandchildren are sick, even when I am nowhere near them, I transmit bounteous messages of recovery. If they are bullied, I become white hot with indignation. I spend time with them and start wondering about their talents, the joys in their life. I try to listen rather than question. I worry about things like their teeth. Will the front ones stick out just like mine and will anything be done about it? And then, the realisation of powerlessness. The humility that comes when your daughter cheerfully says, 'Butt out, lady. You've had your turn, now it's mine.'

She's right, I have had my turn, and while I might want to give her good advice, even when I suspect it's tedious, I also know she has friends to give her good advice, just as I had friends. During the early stages, every time I butted in, I risked stripping her competence by barging in with mine. Not that there's any risk of that nowadays. Her competence outshines mine.

I knew I would love my grandchildren, and hopefully like them, but I did not know that they would give me so much enjoyment to the point that I sometimes appear besotted. And I am. I enjoy spoiling them. Giving them permission while they're with me to break the rules. So that round about the time Odessa challenged my wrinkles, I asked her what was the naughtiest thing she could imagine herself doing. Her eyes widened.

'Sitting on your roof, with no clothes on, and eating the most enormous hugest tub of chocolate ice-cream.' Pause. 'You can come too.'

And then I thought sadly about my own maternal grandmother, Florence, who was usually known as 'Florrie', an abbreviation she abhorred. Florrie, and especially Florence, would have fainted at the thought of sitting anywhere in public without any clothes, especially a rooftop. As for eating ice-cream out of a tub, with no napkin, no spoon, that would have outraged all her sensibilities about class, gentility and good behaviour. She was a woman trapped in the middle class conformities of her age, whom my brother and I scarcely knew and never understood.

The grandmothers of my English childhood gave forth images of piety and prissiness. Florence was a lavender and lace woman who said—interminably—that you could always tell a woman's breeding by her gloves. Women of breeding, she said, wore gloves from Paris. They were seamed on the inside, *never* on the outside. Why I should have remembered this piece of useless and snobbish information for nearly seventy years, I can't imagine, but it stayed with me. Just like me with my own grandchildren, my grandmother corrected our pronunciation, and would have turned pale at the sound of 'haitch' or the word 'youse'. So that while I don't give a fig about the way anyone wears their gloves—if they wear gloves—I do care about pronunciation. As Odessa knows only too well.

Florence wore longish pale grey or mauve skirts and jackets, hats that were usually veiled and, of course, gloves. When she kissed us on the cheek with puckered lips, her ivory skin felt papery thin and soft. Much of the time she lived with a perpetual anxiety that my grandfather, James Montague Baynes—known as 'Bim'—would misbehave. Bim was a solidly built man, shorter than my grandmother; he carried an ivory-topped cane, wore panama hats in summer and he made us laugh.

Bim had the authority of a man who had made a great deal of money. In fact, for a while, he was immensely rich. He owned several large properties in the city of London, and a printing works that produced bank notes for a number of countries in Eastern Europe. But with the advent of the First World War, Bim's best customers and all their currencies were destined to memory. As for the prime real estate, it was heavily mortgaged, insufficiently insured, and bombed to the ground in the Second World War.

Bim was a trickster. He played card tricks, made handkerchiefs come out of our ears, and one Easter, even produced a live rabbit from under a table napkin. It hopped off the table into my grandmother's pale grey lap, leaving little pellets in its wake as she made small, high noises of protest.

Bim told rhymes. 'Say after me very quickly,' he would say, '"I slit the sheet, the sheet slitteth me, the sheet that was slitten was slitten by me."'

'Faster, faster,' he urged as we innocently shouted out loud, 'I shit the sheet, the sheet shitteth me, the sheet that was shitten, was shitten by me.'

'Bim, you are so vulgar,' protested Florence in a voice that trembled with shock and horror.

And now I am remembering how my brother John and I would vainly try to get more involvement with our grandparents by tipping off their hats as they strode down the cobbled streets of Hove to Sunday morning church. We used to perch ourselves at vantage points some height above the roadway, crouching behind bushes, and wielding two long forked sticks.

'Your go, Anne. Silly duffer. You missed.'

I always missed. But then so did John. One day however we scored, and my grandmother's hat went rolling down the road like a dinner plate as she let out little squeaks of surprise and fear. We ran away as fast as we could, both feeling ashamed.

My other grandparents, my paternal ones, died before I was born. And so all I had were brief and shadowy images of the grandparents I knew. Bim doing tricks. Florence disapproving. And then one day, long after they, too, had died, unexpected pieces of information came to light, gleaned from cousins whom we had lost touch with and found again only a short while ago. This was the information that helped me make sense of my grandmother's life. It was a story filled with poignancy.

It seems that in the late 1890s, when Florence was young and beautiful, she worked as a journalist in London, and was one of the first women allowed to use the British Museum Reading Room. The family story says she was *the* first, but hey, let's not be too exact. In the Reading Room, so the story goes, she had an African admirer who gave her a wide gold ring, handsomely engraved with intricate markings that I later discovered were signs of the zodiac. I still have the ring. I have lost it twice, but I always find it again.

Once, in the sixties, when I was filming a story about the first all-women builders' labourers' team, I spotted that the team leader was wearing an identical ring. It had belonged to her grandfather who had bought it in Africa and given it to her grandmother, who gave it to her mother, who gave it to her. Two grandmothers. Two mothers. Two grand-daughters. Two gold rings from Africa, each one lending credence to the story of the other. So how do I link this new and early image of Florence as an independent young woman journalist, one of the first of her kind, with the grandmother I knew as a child—fussy, anxious, inhibited?

The story continues: in 1899, at the beginning of the Boer War and only a short while before the founding of the Commonwealth of Australia, Florence is travelling by train from London to Leeds. We don't know why she makes this journey. We do know she is alone, sitting in a first class railway carriage, and possibly reading a book or writing. Enter a businessman, my grandfather Bim. He is charming, funny, persuasive. He seduces her. I presume that at some stage he draws the blinds and locks the carriage door. Did she know him before this? We don't know.

What we do know is that, nine months later, Florence gives birth to her first child, Barbara—who later becomes my mother. Bim has married Florence and they are living in style in London's Hampstead Heath, where they have servants, horse-drawn carriages and plenty of money. Three more children follow, all boys. Florence goes to church every Sunday; Bim refuses. Florence's life epitomises social propriety and success. Bim continues to make money.

Their four children also live in style but, as they grow up, they notice that at regular intervals their father keeps disappearing. They decide he must have a mistress, tucked away in some exotic place. He is often away for several days at a time and never explains where he is going. Florence doesn't ask. She becomes increasingly anxious and unhappy.

Many years pass and Bim and Florence have retired to the English seaside town of Hove, in Sussex. By now, Bim has lost all his money and they are poor. One day they post four invitations to a wedding. Theirs. My mother and her three brothers arrive in a state of shock and bewilderment.

Bim, who is in his eighties by now, hands out drinks and enjoys the drama.

'I was never legally married to your mother,' he announces. 'I was already married. I am a bigamist. Ha! And you children are therefore bastards.'

Florence weeps.

The explanation then becomes more touching than cruel. My grandfather was indeed already married at the time he met and seduced my grandmother. His wife had schizophrenia in the days before there was any effective medication. She was locked away in a mental asylum somewhere in the north of England—a looney bin, said Bim—and there she remained until she died. Meantime, he had changed his name from Burnley to Baynes and somehow or other bigamously married Florence. It appears he was known as Burnley in the north of England, and Baynes in the south.

Florence marries Bim at Hove Registry Office. It is summer so he wears his panama hat—a new one—and carries his cane. She is dressed in blue and wears white kid gloves, which I am sure were seamed on the inside, and not on the outside.

At the weekend, a photograph appears in England's leading trashy newspaper, *The News of the World*, along with the following headlines:

GRANDPOP MARRIES GRANDMA.
A WHOPPER SURPRISE!

In my grandmother's days, living 'in sin' as it was then described, was instant social death—unless you happened to be a member of the aristocracy when you could get away with more or less anything. Did this account for my grandmother's increasing states of anxiety and her depression? Did she fear that, one day, someone would discover she had four children and wasn't legally married? Worse, that Bim would be labelled a bigamist and go to jail?

Whatever the answers, it's a story that explains something of how Florence changed from being a free-spirited, independent young woman to a woman wracked by fearfulness. It also points up the changes that have happened within three generations. Nowadays, in the culture in which I live, there would be little chance and little reason for my grandchildren not knowing, at least in broad outline, the major pathways and events in my life. Even the state of my wrinkles.

Grandmothers are living longer nowadays. When my mother was born, in the year 1900, the average life expectancy for women was forty-six years, forty-five for men. Today, in 2009, it is eighty-four for women, seventy-nine for men. Many, many more of us are out there in the world. We are independent. We have professions, go out to work, mind children, struggle to get an education, go deep sea diving, break through barriers of medicine and science, toil to save our land, feed our starving grandchildren if all other adults in the family have died from AIDS, run major corporations, fight for human rights.

Grandmothers of the Plaza de Mayo challenged the ruthless dictatorship of Pinochet that ruled Argentina from 1976 to 1983, and risked their lives in protests outside the presidential palace as they demanded the truth about 'the disappeared children of Argentina'—theirs and others. They appear outside the palace to this day, still seeking the truth.

Jewish grandmothers patrol West Bank checkpoints to help prevent Israeli soldiers abusing Palestinian soldiers and civilians as they cross the borders. When an Israeli soldier called one of these women 'a Palestinian whore', she asked him two questions: 'Do you really think that a woman my age has a chance at that profession? And would you say what you said to me to your grandmother?' The soldier said nothing, but was embarrassed. A week later, he apologised.

I give these random examples to show how much has changed since my own grandmother was alive, even though there always have been outstanding examples of women who led the way—women like Rosa Parks, or Emmeline Pankhurst and the suffragettes. Something else is radically different and makes me angry, even though I try to maintain calm. When I was a child, humans only had the capacity to kill each other. Now we are able to kill the world. Either quickly, with nuclear, chemical and biological warfare. Or more slowly, as the world heats up. How will our grandchildren cope with the catastrophes that we are forcing upon them? Will they have time to learn from our mistakes?

One evening in 2003, I was watching news of an American bombing raid over Iraq. One of my grand-children unexpectedly slipped into the room before I had time to change the channel. It was the four-year-old, staring at footage of a little girl about her own age, lying in rubble, covered in blood and screaming, a child's high-pitched cry of terror and pain.

'Oh!' whispered my grand-daughter. 'She's only a little kid, Anne, how could they do that to a little kid?'

Later that night, I walked to the beach and watched waves hurl themselves against the rocks. No stars. No moon. Sea spray flashing like phosphorus bombs. And all the while my grandchild's question reverberating in my head. 'How could they do that to a little kid?'

I wanted to remember my answer. I could only remember my shame.

Contributors

Caitlin ADAMS, a graduate of Bard College and Columbia University, is a writer, editor and visual artist. She has been writing since she was a child, inspired and encouraged by her mother, the Australian author Glenda Adams, who died on 11 July 2007. Caitlin's story is dedicated to her mother. Her current blog, *When Time Meets Eternity*, can be read at http://time-meets-eternity.blogspot.com/. Caitlin was born in New York City and is a dual citizen of the United States and Australia. She has two sons—Isaac and Asher—and lives with her husband, Gary Cutler, and their dog, Sydney, in Cheverly, Maryland, in the United States.

Shalini AKHIL is an Indo-Fijian, Melbourne-based writer who has dabbled in stand-up comedy and is not afraid of hyphens. She's had short pieces published in *Meanjin, Girls' Night In 4, Sleepers Anthology*, *Silverfish New Writing 7, Growing up Asian in Australia* and *The Age A2*. Her first novel, *The Bollywood Beauty,* was published by Penguin Australia, and she's currently working on her second. You can find her online at www.shaliniakhil.com.

Robin BARKER is a grandmother, nurse and the author of two parenting tomes, *Baby Love* and *The Mighty Toddler*, and various other short fiction and non-fiction stories published in anthologies and magazines. She lives surrounded by her family in Sydney, near a famous beach where she swims out beyond the break most days. Robin is grateful for the invitation to contribute to this anthology and loved having the opportunity to transfer childhood glimpses of her grandmothers' lives and the mood of the times in which they lived onto paper.

Many Australians say they've grown up with **Angela CATTERNS**. She's had a diverse media career in film, TV and radio and has broadcast nationally, in Sydney, in country NSW, in Washington DC and most recently, online. You may remember her from *Simon Townsend's Wonder World!*, *Mornings* on Triple J, the *National Evening Show* on ABC Radio, *Breakfast* on 702 ABC Sydney, where she reached Number 1 in the ratings, or the *Breakfast Show* on vega fm in Sydney. Most recently she and fellow broadcaster Wendy Harmer have been podcasting with a sixteen-part series called *Is It Just Me …?* She's always harboured a desire to write and years ago a selection of her poems was published in an anthology of Australian women poets.

Eva COX was born Eva Hauser in Vienna in 1938, and was soon declared stateless by Hitler. So she grew up as a refugee in England until 1946, and arrived in Australia aged ten. These early experiences politicised her, and she remains an active and irrepressible advocate for making more civil societies. She still happily claims the feminist label through a patchy lateral career as academic, advocate, adviser and researcher, and raising her daughter as a sole parent. She fitted in the 1995 ABC Boyer lectures on a Truly Civil Society, activism, Humanist of the Year and an AO, and is now delighted to move to the next generation.

In a long and adventurous life, **Anne DEVESON** has been head of the Australian Film, Television and Radio School; worked on human rights issues around the world; won three media Peace prizes for her films in Africa; and helped change the face of mental illness in Australia. Her books include the internationally acclaimed *Tell Me I'm Here*, the story of her son's struggles with schizophrenia; *Lines in the Sand*, a novel set in Rwanda during the genocide; and *Resilience*, published by Allen & Unwin and broadcast on the ABC. Anne is an Officer of the Order of Australia.

Michele DI'BARTOLO's first book *The Sicilian Kitchen*, published by Penguin in 2008, is part family memoir, travelogue and cookbook, and was shortlisted for the manuscript award in the 2006 Queensland Premier's Literary Awards. Michele has spent time in both Sicily and London but currently lives in Brisbane where she works as a lawyer. As with many Italian families the role of the grandmother looms large and provides many loving and thought-provoking stories.

Sara DOWSE is an author, editor and essayist who in the 1970s was head of the Office of Women's Affairs. Her last novel, *Digging*, appeared in 1996 and two years later she moved to Canada. She returned to Australia in 2004, mainly to be with her grandchildren.

Arabella EDGE read English Literature at Bristol University in the UK and came out to Australia in 1992. Her first novel, *The Company*, won the best first book in the 2001 Commonwealth Writers' Prize in the South East Asia and South Pacific Region and was shortlisted for the 2001 Miles Franklin Award. Her second novel, *The God of Spring*, was published in 2005. She now lives on Tasmania's east coast. Arabella's grandmothers were very different but both had a tremendous influence on her early life.

Kerry GREENWOOD is a solicitor for Victoria Legal Aid, and has written forty-six novels and several collections.

She was taught many things by her grandmothers. She internalised the skills of sewing and mending and cooking, although rather failed at being a lady. But she really appreciated her grandmothers while she had them, and would have been immensely poorer without their care and attention. Now she is approaching their age, she appreciates them more.

Marion HALLIGAN's books include *Spider Cup*, *Lovers' Knots*, *Wishbone*, *The Golden Dress*, *The Fog Garden*, *The Point*, *The Apricot Colonel*, a number of collections of short stories and a children's book. *Eat My Words*, *Cockles of the Heart* and *The Taste of Memory* are books of autobiography, travel and food. Her next novel is *Valley of Grace*. In 2006 she was awarded an AM. But the most exciting thing to happen of late is the birth of a grandchild, a beautiful little girl called Bianca Lucy. So she is a grandmother now too.

Ruby LANGFORD GINIBI is a proud elder of the Bundjalung people. Her published work includes *Don't Take Your Love to Town*, *Real Deadly*, *My Bundjalung People* and *Haunted by the Past*. Her most recent book, *All My Mob*, was published by UQP in 2007. In 2006 Ruby was presented with the Australia Council for the Arts Writers' Emeritus Award in recognition of her achievements. Ruby bore nine children, who she raised mostly on her own, and has survived the deaths of three of them. She is a loving grandmother to twenty-one and a great-grandmother to fifteen.

Gabrielle LORD, BA (Hons) has worked at many jobs, including teaching, peach picking and packing, brick-cleaning, selling, market-gardening and nine years as an Employment Officer. She's written fifteen novels: *Fortress*, *Tooth and Claw*, *Jumbo*, *Salt*, *Whipping Boy*, *Bones*, *The Sharp End*, *Death Delights*, *Feeding the Demons*, *Lethal Factor*, *Baby Did a Bad Bad Thing*, *Dirty Weekend*, *Spiking the Girl*, *Shattered* and *Monkey Undercover* (young adult), as well as journalistic pieces and other non-fiction works. She's currently engaged in writing a young adult, twelve-volume crime thriller series, *Conspiracy 365*, to be released monthly beginning next October, which has already been sold overseas. Her interest in grandmothering began very passionately with the birth of her grand-daughters, Cassie Rose and Georgia Gabrielle. Cassie's read Book 1 'January' of the thriller series. Her response? 'Yia-Yia, I *clinged* to it!' What better could a writer hear?

Julie McCROSSIN talks to people for a living. She also presents a travel program for Qantas and writes for the ABC magazine *Life Etc.* Julie presented *Life Matters* on ABC Radio National for five years and was a team leader on *Good News Week* on Network Ten and ABC TV. Since 1983, she has presented many ABC Radio National programs, including *The Coming Out Show*, *Background Briefing* and *Arts National*, as well as stints on ABC Rural Radio and 702 ABC Sydney. Julie has worked as a TV reporter for both the Sydney Gay and Lesbian Mardi

Gras and ANZAC Day—and she's thrilled to live in a country where it is possible to do both. But her proudest media moment was her appearance on ABC TV's *Play School* as a silent clown called Plain Jane. Julie has qualifications in the arts, education and law. She is the co-editor (with Kerrie Jean Ross) of *Forever Yours: Australia's Hidden Love Letters*.

Lorraine McGEE-SIPPEL is a Yorta Yorta, Anglo-Celtic woman who was taken from her Aboriginal mother at birth and reunited with her biological family in 1981. Lorraine's autobiography, *Hey Mum, What's a Half-caste?* was shortlisted for the David Unaipon Award in the 2006 and 2007 Queensland Premier's Literary Awards, and published by Magabala Books in 2009. She has performed her work at various venues and her writing appears in a number of publications, including the *Koori Mail*. In 2008 Lorraine received the inaugural Yabun Elder of the Year Award for her work and contribution to reconciliation.

Jennifer MILLS is the author of the novel, *The Diamond Anchor* (UQP, 2009) and several award-winning poems and short stories. In 2008 Jennifer was awarded the Marian Eldridge Award for Emerging Women Writers. She lives in Alice Springs where she is hard at work on her second novel, with the assistance of a grant from the Australia Council for the Arts.

Eileen NASEBY was born in Haifa in 1943. At the age of ten she emigrated to Australia with her mother and stepfather. Married to the painter David Naseby in the mid-1960s, Eileen raised four children before establishing Australia's leading stock footage film library Film World. With Film World and Murdoch Books, Eileen produced the Australian Memories series of photographic books, showcasing images from the Cinesound Movietone Archive. In 2006 Murdoch Books published *Ursula—A Voyage of Love and Danger*, Eileen's biography of her mother Ursula Hall. Eileen has received several fellowships to Varuna—The Writers' House in the Blue Mountains of NSW, and is now at work on a novel.

Kristina OLSSON is a Brisbane-based writer and journalist. Her second novel, *The China Garden*, was published in March 2009 by UQP. She is the author of *Kilroy Was Here* (Random House, 2005), the biography of prison activist Debbie Kilroy, and the novel *In One Skin* (UQP, 2001). Her work has appeared widely in newspapers and journals including *Griffith Review*. She is grandmother to Amber and Antonio and is hopeful of many more.

Paddy O'REILLY is the author of a collection of short stories, *The End of the World*; a novel, *The Factory*; and a novella, 'Deep Water' (in *Love and Desire,* ed. Cate Kennedy). She spent several years in Japan working as a copywriter and translator, and now lives in country Victoria.

Annette SHUN WAH is descended from at least three generations of hoarders. That's probably because there was a shopkeeper in every generation, and the queen of these was her paternal grandmother, Sam Moy. So even though Annette is a writer, actor and broadcaster, with no reason to keep inventory, be assured she'll always have ample supplies of the necessities of life (soap powder, soy sauce and toilet paper).

52